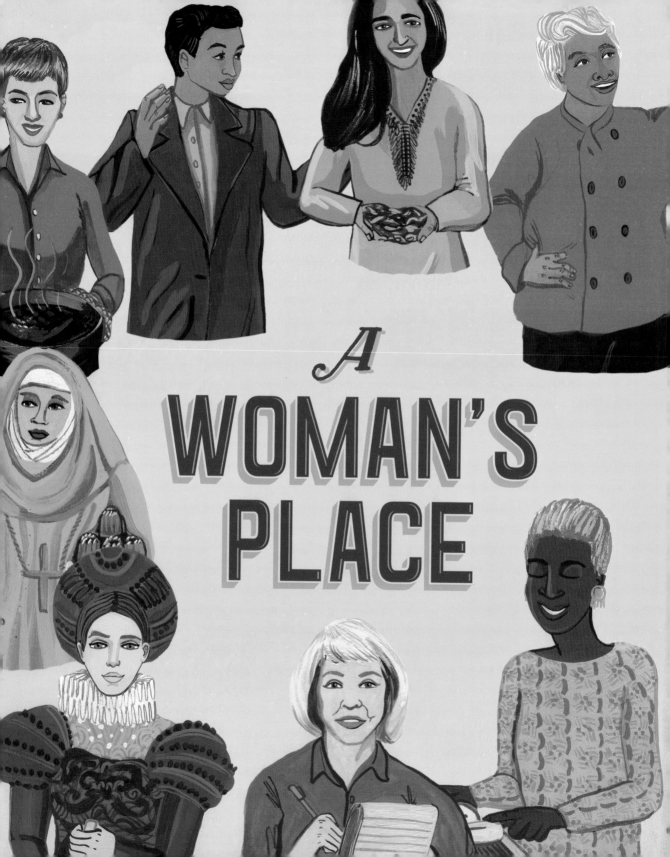

A WOMAN'S PLACE

THE INVENTORS, RUMRUNNERS,
LAWBREAKERS, SCIENTISTS & SINGLE MOMS WHO
*CHANGED THE WORLD
WITH FOOD*

DEEPI AHLUWALIA & STEF FERRARI

ILLUSTRATED BY *Jessica Olah*

LITTLE, BROWN AND COMPANY

NEW YORK   BOSTON   LONDON

Little, Brown and Company
Hachette Book Group
1290 Avenue of the Americas, New York, NY 10104
littlebrown.com

First Edition: March 2019

Little, Brown and Company is a division of Hachette Book Group, Inc.
The Little, Brown name and logo are trademarks of Hachette Book Group, Inc.

The publisher is not responsible for websites (or their content)
that are not owned by the publisher.

The Hachette Speakers Bureau provides a wide range of authors
for speaking events. To find out more, go to hachettespeakersbureau.com
or call (866) 376-6591.

Illustrations by Jessica Olah

Interior design and hand lettering by Laura Palese

ISBN 978-0-316-45224-3
LCCN 2018954876

10 9 8 7 6 5 4 3 2 1

WOR

Printed in the United States of America

TO THE LADIES
WHO
GIVE ME STRENGTH

my mother, Ramjit Kaur, and my warrior princesses,
Paavni Kaur and Suhaavi Kaur

—D.A.

TO ASSUNTA & ROSIE

my own personal trailblazers—in the kitchen
and far beyond

—S.F.

Conte[nts]

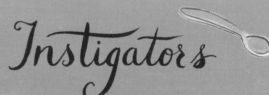

nts

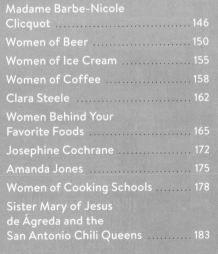

Inventors

Introduction
OUR PLACE

*T*HIS BOOK BEGAN WITH A QUESTION: If a woman's place has always been in the kitchen, then why does culinary history read like the guest list of some old boys' club? Women were the stars of our holiday traditions and romanticized tales of home cooking passed down through generations, but a glance at the front pages of food publications, lists of the world's best restaurants, or even our corner bistro revealed a different face of the food industry: men. Women may be depicted slaving over the proverbial (or literal) hot stove (before putting dinner on the table in a perfectly pressed dress), but rarely are we considered fit for jobs in professional kitchens. Men have long been the ones holding the pens that recorded history, but so often it was women wielding the knives—not to mention the spatulas, the spoons, and the know-how. So where were they?

Between the two of us authors, we've racked up four decades of industry experience in culinary schools and kitchens of all kinds, in cities all over the country, and in just about every post from line cook to pastry chef to beer sommelier before settling into food writing, photography, and documentary filmmaking. We've seen almost everything the food world has to offer, except for one thing: female representation.

But we knew that women had been there all along, and when we looked, we found countless women who changed the world of food. And we also found women who used food to change the world.

We learned that women made the peanut butter and jelly sandwich and the modern-day doughnut, but we also learned that they made history. Some used food for protest, as a tool to make people *feel* something—pride, outrage, or a call to action. For these women, food was political in surprising and subtle ways: in making freshly churned ice cream a treat for everyone regardless of class; in a recipe for Chinese stir-fry that gave expatriate families a taste of home; in a fried chicken sandwich that financed a community of civil rights activists.

But these women (and girls) weren't just sugar and spice—they were full of fire. In these pages, you'll meet rumrunners and lawbreakers, women who weren't afraid to challenge the status quo, for money or love, or for the good of humanity. They made it their mission to move the needle, rules be damned. And these innovators, instigators, and inventors made contributions to science, technology, culture, and politics that reached far beyond the dinner table.

A Woman's Place is about telling their stories, giving these fierce women a face and a voice. It's about changing the narrative about women in the food world. It's about demonstrating that if a woman found herself in a kitchen, it wasn't because she was forced there; more often than not, she fought her way in. It's not about rewriting history—it's about uncovering what's been there all along. It's about due credit, in the kitchen and on our dinner tables. It's about inspiring members of a new generation to embrace their own creativity, to transcend their own circumstances, to take energy from what came before, and to use their skill—in any profession—to change the world.

It's about giving women their rightful place—in the kitchen.

Innov

VERTAMAE SMART-GROSVENOR
Vibration
Cooking
THE TRAVEL NOTES OF A
GEECHEE GIRL

ators

THESE RESOURCEFUL
WOMEN WERE HUNGRY FOR
SOMETHING BETTER.

A
DOMESTIC
COOK BOOK
FOR THE KITCHEN

MRS MALINDA RUSSELL
AN EXPERIENCED COOK

Catherine de' Medici

1519-1589

WHEN YOU SIT DOWN to eat at your favorite French bistro, enjoy the formal ceremony of a fancy restaurant, or even use a fork, you have a woman to thank. Born in 1519, the daughter of an Italian statesman and a French princess, Catherine de' Medici was sent at the age of fourteen to marry the heir to the French throne, the future Henry II. A royal engagement may sound like a dream, but Catherine's marriage was hardly the stuff of fairy tales. France, her new home, was less than enthusiastic about the match and became even more critical of the new queen when she failed to produce an heir. Henry quickly and publicly took a mistress and allowed Catherine very little influence in matters of state. In lieu of motherhood and

governance, she found purpose elsewhere, taking inspiration from the flowering of culture in Italy later known as the Renaissance, which began in her hometown of Florence, and establishing herself as a patron of the arts. The culinary arts were no exception, and what she was unable to accomplish in politics, she made up for in the royal kitchen.

Catherine introduced Italian ingredients that would go on to inform much of French cuisine—from foods like artichokes, peas, spinach, lettuce, and broccoli, to aspics, veal, sweetbreads, and truffles, to sweeter things like cream puffs, custards, cakes, sherbets, and ices, not to mention, of course, pasta. Even some quintessential French dishes, like duck *à l'orange*, are said to have been brought from Italy at Catherine's behest.

Beyond food, Catherine conveyed Italian custom and style to her new country's tableside. Now it may seem as if the French invented table manners, but in the sixteenth century, it would have been more common to see French nobility digging into their dinner with bare hands. Before Catherine introduced the fork, an Italian invention, dishes were primarily eaten as finger foods; stews and similar hearty dishes were still served with a knife and a slice of bread, to be speared and scooped. Just try to imagine a fancy French restaurant today that wouldn't be more than a little horrified by that practice.

It's hard to say for certain how many items made their way across borders as a result, but Catherine's culinary influence is indisputable. By uniting the heritages of France and Italy, she helped lay the foundation of French cuisine, widely considered to be the first fine-dining culture.

Lena Richard

1892 – 1950

DECADES BEFORE JULIA CHILD became synonymous with domestic prowess, there was Lena Richard: the first African-American culinary icon. Through her kitchen skills and business savvy, Lena's empire grew to include cookbooks, restaurants, and a television show. And she did it all during the height of segregation and racial prejudice in America.

In the era of Jim Crow, "opportunity" was hard to come by. Racist laws disenfranchised and humiliated African Americans, and careers for women of color were mostly limited to domestic work. Lena began earning a salary around 1906 in the kitchen of Alice Nugent Vairin, a socialite who nonetheless recognized her gift for cooking. Alice offered to fund Lena's culinary education—first at a local New Orleans cooking school, then at the Fannie Farmer cooking school in Boston—and Lena leapt at the chance.

Innovators

But she already had what it took. "When I got up there," she said of her experience at the legendary cooking school, "I found out in a hurry they can't teach me much more than I know...when it comes to cooking meats, stews, soups and sauces; we Southern cooks have Northern cooks beat by a mile." Emboldened, Lena returned home to launch her catering business. She was so successful that she was able to open a sweet shop, and eventually her own cooking school, where even white socialites lined up for her demos. Her 1939 self-published work, *Lena Richard's Cook Book*, caught the attention of publishing house Houghton Mifflin, which reissued the book under the title *New Orleans Cook Book* as a singular collection of Creole recipes.

Lena left New Orleans to head restaurants in New York and Colonial Williamsburg, started a frozen-food line with her daughter, and launched two restaurants, including Lena's Eatery in 1941. The latter was famous for its integrated dining room, where blacks and whites ate together in deliberate violation of forced segregation laws. Lena hosted her own cooking show, decades before Julia Child became the first chef to appear on live TV.

Despite the devaluing of black lives by the world around her, Lena knew her self-worth. Her success was a source of hometown pride, and she was living proof for countless African Americans of what they could achieve if they were empowered to pursue their own dreams.

Eugénie ("La Mère") Brazier

1895 - 1977

IN THE EARLY TWENTIETH CENTURY, the in-crowd of Paris's haute cuisine was a boys' club. But it was Eugénie Brazier, a tough-as-nails farm girl from the countryside, who beat out the boys to become one of the most decorated chefs in French history.

Raised in rural Certines, Eugénie learned uncomplicated country dishes—soups, breads, tarts, and tripe—at her mother's side. When she became a mother herself, she moved to Lyon to find work and became an apprentice in the all-female kitchen of Françoise Fillioux. There, she learned to cook with truffles and foie gras, larks, ortolans, and partridges—luxury ingredients Eugénie learned to handle like a boss. She experimented with

Innovators

ingredients and tweaked recipes, at times butting heads with Françoise, a celebrated chef in her own right. Eventually, Eugénie left Françoise to head another kitchen, opening her own restaurant in Lyon at the age of twenty-six.

Eugénie was a master of simplicity and perfectionism, taking basic ingredients and turning them into culinary symphonies. Her dishes, from artichokes with foie gras to truffled chicken—known as Chicken in Half-Mourning due to the veil-like appearance of black truffles tucked under the skin—were without gimmick. Despite her meager education, she had a shrewd business sense and knew the value of strong relationships, from faithful vendors on whom she relied for superior ingredients to regular guests who became close friends.

A sturdy woman, she commanded her two restaurants—the Lyon establishment and one in the foothills of the Alps—with a stern hand, hot temper, and exacting standards. Eugénie was so committed to quality that she spent a week in prison for repeatedly ignoring mandatory wartime rations. Over decades, word of her cooking spread, attracting aspiring chefs seeking her mentorship, including the legendary Paul Bocuse, who arrived at her doorstep barely out of his teens.

Eugénie was the first chef to ever receive six Michelin stars: three for each restaurant. She let the culinary patriarchy know that fine cooking was not just a man's world and is still revered as the mother—*la mère*—of modern French cuisine.

Encarnación Pinedo

1848–1902

TODAY, MEXICAN FOOD MAY be one of the most popular cuisines in the world, with taco trucks as internationally ubiquitous as the golden arches or Coca-Cola cans. But in 1898, when Encarnación Pinedo published her cookbook *El Cocinero Español* (*The Spanish Cook*), the foods of Mexico were—much like its people—underrepresented and unappreciated.

Though her family's wealth was dramatically reduced following the Mexican-American War, the Pinedos, land-owning Californios (Mexican Americans living in what is now California), still provided Encarnación with a strong education. Born in 1848, the year California moved from Mexican control to that of the United States, Encarnación was arguably one of the first bicultural figures in American history. Her book is a reflection of that experience, with ingredients from the New World, like tomatoes, squash, and

chiles, as well as European ones like shallots and almonds, capers and spices. Recipes span cultures from French to Italian to German, evidence of historical influence and migration across borders, oceans, and eras.

Her recipes embraced a cross section of cultural influences, but Encarnación wasn't exactly hiding her disdain for the English-speaking world that had wreaked havoc on her family's life. With dishes like *Huevos Hipócritas*, or "Hypocrite's Eggs" (a breakfast of ham and eggs beloved by white Europeans)—or through passages in which she refers to foods of "the Englishman" as "the most insipid and tasteless that one can imagine"—it's obvious that her contempt was as much for colonialism as flavorless food.

El Cocinero Español was given new life in the early 1990s when then *Los Angeles Times* food critic Ruth Reichl called it the earliest iteration of modern Mexican food and the precursor to California cuisine. In fact, its global influence and tendency toward vegetable-forward, ingredient-driven dishes that highlight fresh herbs, fruits, and wood-fire grilling techniques would probably have made Alice Waters and Wolfgang Puck proud. The book was edited and translated into English by Dan Strehl, co-founder of Culinary Historians of Southern California, and released in 2003 by the University of California Press as *Encarnación's Kitchen*.

Maybe Encarnación knew in 1898 that she was writing an important collection—one that revealed the new Latina world through her own eyes. But she had no way of knowing she was articulating challenges her bicultural kin continue to face more than a century later. Today, her words still provide not only foundational recipes for present-day cuisine, but priceless context to the modern Latin American experience.

Esther Eng

1914-1970

FAMED *NEW YORK TIMES* food critic Craig Claiborne had only one complaint about Bo Bo's, the acclaimed Chinatown restaurant owned by Esther Eng, powerhouse film director turned restaurateur: it was too damn hard to get a table. Regardless of her medium, no matter what she decided to do, Esther did it *her* way, and in the process redefined the lines of race, gender, sexuality, and culture.

Growing up in San Francisco, young Esther was totally hooked on the vibrant arts scene of the Chinese community. Fortunately, that interest ran in the family. Her father founded a production company, to use films to

promote Chinese culture. Esther made movies in both Chinese and English, and helped to establish Chinese opera in the United States. Bruce Lee even made his film debut as an infant in one of her early movies, 1941's *Golden Gate Girl*.

Esther, who lived openly as a lesbian, moved to New York City, where she joined up with a network of actors unable to leave the United States due to China's new communist regime. Esther saw an opportunity to help her struggling, stranded community and opened a restaurant where Chinese-American actors could find reliable employment and work on their English. She named it Bo Bo's, for one such friend.

But Bo Bo's wasn't a charity project; the restaurant received raves. And while it was frequented by high society, Esther didn't compromise her culture. Bo Bo's served authentic Chinese dishes—if pricey ones, with an emphasis on lobster and steak—instead of the more common Americanized interpretations. Between 1950 and 1967, Esther opened five restaurants, where she could often be found among the crowds of diners, rocking the suits and short haircuts then considered acceptable only for men. Esther lived her life openly and honestly, defying societal expectations and always being herself.

Esther was a passionate, creative, and courageous fighter for her culture and community. She challenged the status quo as a woman in not one but two male-dominated industries. And she did it all by pushing the boundaries of what it meant to be bicultural, queer, and female, never hiding who she truly was.

CHINESE FIVE-SPICE
BRAISED BEEF SHORT RIBS

SERVES 4

EQUIPMENT: 4½-quart Dutch oven, tinfoil

3 pounds beef short ribs, cut into 4-ounce portions

1 teaspoon kosher salt

1 tablespoon ginger, grated

1 teaspoon five-spice powder

½ teaspoon chili-garlic sauce

½ teaspoon crushed red pepper

¼ teaspoon mustard powder

¼ teaspoon Santa Maria seasoning (available online)

1 teaspoon canola oil

1½ tablespoons garlic, minced

2 cups water

¼ cup rice vinegar

1 teaspoon mirin

1½ teaspoons sesame oil

3 tablespoons orange juice

12 green onion bulbs (save stalks for garnish)

5 medium carrots, peeled and cut into 2-inch-long batons

2 lemongrass cores, cut in half lengthwise, minced

½ teaspoon hoisin sauce

Rub beef short ribs with salt to dry-brine. Let sit 3 hours in fridge. After 3 hours, combine ginger, five-spice powder, chili-garlic sauce, crushed red pepper, mustard powder, and Santa Maria seasoning. Rub mixture on ribs.

Preheat oven to 350°F. Place Dutch oven on stovetop over medium heat. Add canola oil and sauté garlic until lightly browned. Add water, rice vinegar, mirin, sesame oil, orange juice, green onion bulbs, carrots, and lemongrass. Place short ribs in Dutch oven so they're standing vertically. Cover with lid and cook for 2½ hours or until meat falls easily off bone.

Use tongs to remove ribs and vegetables from Dutch oven. In same Dutch oven over medium-high heat, reduce remaining liquid by a third, about 6–8 minutes, and stir in hoisin sauce.

Place braised ribs on bed of jasmine rice. Add vegetables around rice. Spoon reduced sauce over ribs and garnish with chopped green onions.

Vertamae Smart~Grosvenor

1937–2016

Different strokes for different folks.
Do your thing your way.

—VERTAMAE SMART-GROSVENOR

TODAY, CHEFS OF ALL BACKGROUNDS find inspiration in the cuisine of the American South, mining history for its origins and re-creating early dishes, or curating the long-forgotten heirloom rice and corn varieties that once defined its plates. But long before hoppin' John became trendy, Vertamae Smart-Grosvenor chronicled Southern food, inviting those of African

ancestry to claim their rightful place as the founders of American cuisine.

With a lineage that can be traced back to Sierra Leone and the surrounding regions, Vertamae's Gullah Geechee people are the descendants of early American slaves who settled in low-country areas, from Florida to North Carolina to the Georgia coast. During Vertamae's early years in the Gullah Geechee Corridor of South Carolina, her family depended on rice, a staple crop as important to the community of her youth as it had been to colonial planters and the enslaved Africans who worked their fields.

Vertamae loved the arts and itched to see the world, so in the 1950s, when she was nineteen, she saved her pennies for a trip to Paris. There she met the man who would become her husband. The couple moved to New York City, where she pursued her dream of acting and became involved in the Black Arts movement. Though she and her husband later divorced, Vertamae was left with two daughters who remember a home vibrating with life, thanks to her creativity and cooking. A woman who never wanted for talent, she achieved her girlhood goal—and the American dream—of seeing her name in lights with performances as an actress on Broadway. But food always called her back.

In 1970, she published *Vibration Cooking: or, The Travel Notes of a Geechee Girl*. Part diary, part cookbook, it was a seminal text on African-American food and culture. At the time, embracing her Gullah Geechee identity was an act of defiance against a prejudiced society. In the book, Vertamae emphasized the importance of instinct in cooking. "When I cook, I never measure or weigh anything," she told readers. "I cook by vibration." She wasn't afraid to be direct about how the food of her ancestors was being interpreted along lines of

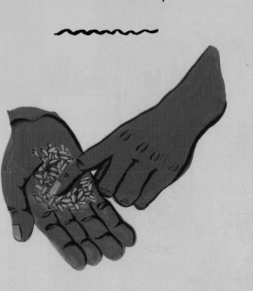

A STAPLE TRAVELS
TO THE STATES

When the slave trade was at its height, women captured from
Africa often fed their fellow slaves in transit and in the New World. These
women preserved the techniques of farming and cooking rice,
and in smuggling African varietals over to America, they made possible
the rice we eat today.

racist and classist power. "White folks always discovering something...after we give it up," she wrote. Fittingly, she also told stories that challenged common beliefs about the food of the African-American diaspora. By including global dishes with influences from Europe and beyond, Vertamae demonstrated that the cooking of the American South could stand proudly among the great cuisines of the world.

In the 1980s, Vertamae began appearing as a regular contributor to National Public Radio, where she examined the anthropology of American food and became a prolific documentarian of African-American culture. Her diverse body of work earned her a James Beard Award for Best Radio Broadcast and, just before her death, in 2016, the Southern Foodways Alliance Craig Claiborne Lifetime Achievement Award.

Vibration Cooking remains a cornerstone of food culture and evidence of African influence on the food Americans eat every day. It was published at a precarious time for African Americans, when the dust of the civil rights movement had only just begun to settle, and the question of what was next was on everyone's mind. Vertamae's work was instrumental in preserving the heritage and history of the African-American experience, but also in providing a strong and fearless voice for its future.

Edna Lewis

1916-2006

THERE'S NOTHING EASY ABOUT changing deeply rooted cultural perceptions. But through simple food and a strong sense of place, Edna Lewis not only altered stereotypical notions of Southern cooking, she forever cemented its importance in American cuisine.

Edna was born in 1916 in Freetown, Virginia, a cooperative rural community founded by her grandfather, an emancipated slave, built on the bonds between families and neighbors. In Freetown, activity revolved around seasonal food. Communities came together to sow and reap, forage and butcher, sharing above all a reverence for the land and its bounty. Edna's

mother and aunt were both excellent cooks and taught Edna what they knew. She also took cues from other women, many of whom worked as domestics and cooks for elite Virginians.

After her father's death, Edna left at the age of sixteen, first for Washington, D.C., then New York. She worked as a seamstress—even stitching dresses for Marilyn Monroe—and became known for intricate African-inspired designs. But Edna found her way back to the comforts of cooking, becoming chef and partner at Café Nicholson, a restaurant on Manhattan's East Side. Word spread of her sublime Southern food: elegant but simple dishes prepared from the heart, like succulent roast chicken with herbs, melt-in-your-mouth filet mignon, and feather-light chocolate soufflé. The café's popularity soared; Tennessee Williams, Truman Capote, Marlon Brando, Marlene Dietrich, Greta Garbo, and Eleanor Roosevelt all took seats at its tables.

In 1972, a collection of popular dishes from Café Nicholson called *The Edna Lewis Cookbook* was published. But it was her second book, *The Taste of Country Cooking*, released four years later, that flung open the doors to authentic Southern cooking, a cuisine made with pure ingredients simply prepared. Encouraged by Knopf editor Judith Jones (page 120), Edna wrote down recipes and memories in her warm and conversational voice. The result was a love letter to Freetown and a lesson in mindfulness. It expressed a philosophy of simple pleasures, being aware of and taking joy in the present moment, and thoughtfully described ideals of slow food and slow living.

To ensure the legacy of Southern cooking, she founded the Society for the Revival and Preservation of Southern Food. Edna was widely celebrated for her work preserving the history of American food and was awarded an honorary PhD in culinary arts from Johnson and Wales University. Her life's work not only altered society's understanding of Southern food, it opened minds and hearts, and inspired a generation of Southern chefs.

HERB-ROASTED CHICKEN & VEGETABLES WITH SAGE BUTTERMILK BISCUITS

SERVES 4

EQUIPMENT: Roasting pan, baster, meat thermometer, sheet pan or baking sheet, parchment paper

HERB-ROASTED CHICKEN & VEGETABLES

1 (4- to 5-pound) chicken

1 medium lemon, quartered

6 cloves garlic, divided

2 tablespoons unsalted butter, melted

4 teaspoons kosher salt, divided

1 teaspoon cracked black pepper, divided

2 tablespoons herbes de Provence

2 fennel bulbs, cut into 1-inch wedges

2 shallots, quartered

1 pound fingerling potatoes, halved, or baby potatoes, quartered

4 large carrots, cut into ½-inch slices

2 tablespoons olive oil

1 cup white wine or sherry

SAGE BUTTERMILK BISCUITS

2 cups all-purpose flour

3 teaspoons baking powder

½ teaspoon baking soda

¾ teaspoon kosher salt

1½ tablespoons ground sage

6 tablespoons cold butter, cubed

1 cup buttermilk, chilled

2 tablespoons butter, melted

Make the Herb-Roasted Chicken & Vegetables: Preheat oven to 500°F.

Pat chicken dry and place in roasting pan greased with olive oil. Stuff lemon quarters and 3 cloves garlic inside cavity of chicken. Coat outside of chicken with melted butter, using hands to rub butter into all crevices. Generously season outside of chicken with half the salt and black pepper, followed by herbes de Provence.

In large mixing bowl, combine remaining garlic (3 cloves) with fennel bulbs, shallots, potatoes, and carrots. Pour olive oil over vegetables and thoroughly mix until all ingredients are coated with oil. Transfer vegetables to roasting pan, arranging them evenly around chicken. Pour white wine or sherry over vegetables and sprinkle with remaining salt (2 teaspoons) and black pepper (½ teaspoon).

Roast chicken for 25 minutes until skin turns golden. Reduce heat to 350°F. Rotate pan and baste chicken and vegetables with liquid in pan. Continue roasting chicken for 40 more minutes, basting every 10 minutes. Chicken will be fully cooked when internal temperature of thigh reads 165°F and juices run clear. Vegetables will be fork-tender. Remove pan from oven and cover with tinfoil. Let chicken rest for 15 minutes before carving. Serve with vegetables.

Make the Sage Buttermilk Biscuits: Line sheet pan or baking sheet with parchment paper. Combine all dry ingredients in bowl and whisk together. Chill mixture in freezer for 5–10 minutes. When dry ingredients are thoroughly cold, dump mixture onto clean work surface. Using dough cutter, pastry cutter, or knife, work quickly to cut cold butter into mixture, until butter is pea-sized. Create well and add buttermilk in two additions, mixing by hand until dough just comes together in shaggy ball. If dough is too wet or dry, add flour or buttermilk in tiny amounts. Don't knead or overwork dough, as this will create excess gluten and warm up butter. Turn dough out onto lightly floured work surface and pat into ¾-inch-thick square, roughly 7 x 7 inches. Fold dough in half and pat down again to ¾-inch thickness. Repeat until dough has been folded five times. After last fold, pat dough into ¾-inch-thick square. With sharp knife, cut dough into nine squares. Transfer squares to parchment-lined pan and brush tops with melted butter. Place pan in freezer for 30 minutes or fridge for 1 hour.

Preheat oven to 425°F.

Place pan on middle rack in oven and bake for 15 minutes, rotating halfway through, until biscuits are golden brown. Transfer biscuits immediately to wire rack to cool.

Pair warm biscuits with Herb-Roasted Chicken or enjoy cooled with a drizzle of honey.

Erna Meyer

TWENTIETH CENTURY

BY THE TIME Dr. Erna Meyer immigrated to Palestine from Germany in 1933, she'd already published several books for homemakers that compared the operation of a home to running a business. But in *How to Cook in Palestine*, she helped her readers, Jewish immigrants to Palestine, establish a unified cuisine.

For people settling in a new land, the flavors of their home are often the first thing they seek to recapture. Food can comfort and transport you to a certain time and place. But "Jewish food" may be the rare cuisine

defined by a *lack* of place. Throughout history, Jewish people were made to hide their beliefs and identity, exiled and forced again and again from their homes. In Erna's book, published in the 1930s by the Women's International Zionist Organization, she adapted traditional Jewish dishes to the ingredients and tools available to her fellow immigrants. Dishes like chopped liver, a staple of the Ashkenazi diet, were modified to use eggplant. Instructions noted the lack of ovens and refrigerators that many Europeans were accustomed to owning, suggesting stovetop preparations instead. Sensitive to the financial conditions of recent immigrants, Erna leaned on potatoes and vegetables over pricier cuts of meat.

Erna's book was about far more than dinner. It was reflective of the greater immigrant experience across cultures—the tension between preservation and integration. She emphasized that recent immigrants "must take an attempt to free our kitchens from European customs which are not applicable to Palestine" and that doing so was "one of the most important means to establishing our roots." Erna's work helped the Jewish diaspora find its identity, as well as the confidence and stability of a new and uniquely Jewish cuisine.

Eva Ekeblad

1724-1786

TODAY, POTATOES MAY BE standard on tables all over the globe for breakfast, dinnertime, and even dessert, but for nearly a century after the humble spud was introduced in Sweden, in 1658, Swedes regarded it as nothing more than animal feed. Then eighteenth-century agronomist (i.e., farm scientist) and countess Eva Ekeblad introduced the nation to the power of the little root—and changed everything.

When she was twenty-two and tending to her husband's estate, Eva grew her own potatoes. Inspired by tales of other countries using the spud for a variety of purposes, she began experimenting. She cooked them, dried

them, pulverized them into a flour that could be used for bread, and distilled them into alcohol. Eva employed the flour as a nontoxic ingredient in cosmetics and even promoted her beloved potato by wearing its flowers in her hair.

Eva's discoveries also provided new ways to sustain hungry populations. Thanks to her advocacy and innovation, the potato became an integral part of the Swedish diet. Her use of potato flour in the production of bread and alcohol helped allow for the preservation of precious grains like rye, wheat, and barley, fighting the frequent famines that plagued her country. Eva became the first female inducted into the Royal Swedish Academy of Sciences, but frustratingly, her membership was later downgraded to an "honorary" acknowledgment, as women weren't allowed to be fully fledged members. Two centuries would pass before the academy recognized another woman. We owe many of the potato dishes we adore to her ingenuity, but Eva's work exposed more than the tater's delicious versatility. Her intellect, curiosity, and pluck gave the Swedish people an indispensable, lifesaving staple.

Malinda Russell

NINETEENTH CENTURY

COOKBOOKS OFFER MORE THAN recipes. They provide a window into a culture and time period, and into a person's life. Malinda Russell's 1866 publication, *Domestic Cook Book: Containing a Careful Selection of Useful Receipts for the Kitchen,* is a historical treasure, as much for its recipes as for its insight into the lives of free African Americans after the Civil War.

Hers is widely believed to be the first cookbook by an African American. Malinda's book—a slim thirty-nine pages privately published in Paw Paw, Michigan—showed there was more to African-American cuisine than just "soul food." In the South, what we know as soul food originated as poverty cooking during the reprehensible era of American slavery, and fried chicken, collard greens, cornbread, and chitlins had since been considered by white audiences the single form of African-American cuisine. But Malinda's book reveals that African Americans cooked internationally and widely: Charlotte

Russe, Irish Potato Custard, and A-La-Mode Beef appear alongside traditional dishes like Sweet Potato Baked Pudding and Chow Chow (a traditional Southern pickled relish). As subsequent cookbooks written by African Americans entered the culinary sphere, they solidified Malinda's cosmopolitan flavor-bending as a norm rather than an outlier.

She was born a free woman in Tennessee and later moved to Lynchburg, Virginia, where she met her husband and started a family. But her happiness was quickly shattered when her husband died four years later, leaving her to provide for their son. She started a laundry service—branding herself the Fashionable Laundress—and apprenticed under another African-American cook, Fannie Steward. Malinda took inspiration from her female mentors in writing her book, in which she credits recipes to her former teacher and also includes a nod to Mary Randolph's 1824 cookbook, *The Virginia Housewife* (page 167).

Her collection of recipes was intended, in part, to share knowledge, but also, after the outbreak of the Civil War forced her to flee Tennessee for Michigan, to earn her enough money to return home. It's not clear if Malinda ever made it; traces of her life in Paw Paw—her last known address—have vanished, possibly destroyed in a fire in 1866.

Though the remainder of her history may be lost to time, Malinda's story shows that cultural narratives are not one-size-fits-all. Her book was an inspiration to generations of black women in the kitchen—some in this very book—who learned that with passion, purpose, and insight, you can write your own ending.

Women of Chinese-American Food

TWENTIETH CENTURY - PRESENT

CECILIA CHIANG When Cecilia Chiang opened the Mandarin in San Francisco, in 1961, she brought the Sichuanese flavors of her youth to American Chinese food.

Cecilia was forced to flee China in 1942 following the Japanese invasion. After briefly living and operating a Chinese restaurant in Tokyo, she relocated to San Francisco, where the population's experience with Chinese food was almost exclusively in Americanized "chop suey houses." Cecilia refused to bend to this interpretation of Chinese food. Initially, she had trouble even securing ingredients from purveyors who didn't approve of her approach—or her gender. But she persisted and confidently sent samples of her food to diners. Soon her restaurant caught the eye of food critics and celebrities, and became a sensation. In fewer than ten years, she outgrew the original space and moved the Mandarin into Ghirardelli Square in 1968. As it

CECILIA CHIANG

JOYCE CHEN

the mandarin

MENU
LO MEIN   CHICKEN
1   15
2   16
3   17
4   18
5   19
6   20
DIM SUM   21
7   22
8   23
9   24
10   25
11   26
12   27
13
14

BUWEI YANG
CHAO

HOW TO COOK
AND EAT
IN CHINESE

expanded, the restaurant became an American institution, much like Chinese food itself. Cecilia wrote several cookbooks and even schooled Julia Child in Chinese cooking.

Cecilia not only established a prominent restaurant but changed the way Chinese food and culture were viewed. The Mandarin was on par with any French or Italian restaurant, upending the perception that Chinese food couldn't fit the fine-dining profile. And, in further proof of her influence on Chinese food's total permeation of American dining culture, Cecilia's son went on to co-found P. F. Chang's, and one of her employees founded Panda Express.

JOYCE CHEN When Joyce Chen opened her first restaurant in Cambridge, Massachusetts, in 1958, it might not have been her intention to change Americans' ideas about Chinese food, but that's exactly what she did. Whether by using the buffet to gently introduce diners to new dishes, or numbering the items on her menu in an attempt to lower the language barrier for her guests—a practice still popular in many Chinese restaurants—Joyce made the food of her homeland more accessible to her American neighbors.

Throughout her impressive career as a restaurateur, entrepreneur, educator, author, and television host, Joyce was a cultural ambassador. Her cookbooks and TV shows made it seem easy to cook Chinese food at home. And while she popularized many touchstones of traditional Chinese-American cuisine, from dim sum to soup dumplings to moo shoo pork, she also played fast and loose with authenticity in favor of accessibility. She made "Peking ravioli" and sometimes called for hamburger meat in her egg rolls (a dish first created to appeal to her children's classmates). Joyce was uniquely aware of what might stop a home cook from tackling her recipes, so she used ingredients familiar and available to them and adopted language that readers, diners, and viewers would recognize.

Her ingenuity extended beyond the kitchen as she built her empire; Joyce patented a flat-bottomed wok design suitable for American stovetops and launched a line of Chinese cooking tools, condiments, and sauces, always with the aim of educating a new audience. For anyone enjoying Chinese food in America (so, everyone in America), her influence is evident in every crispy piece of Peking duck.

BUWEI YANG CHAO Today, it's common practice for immigrants to re-create the food of their homes to comfort themselves, their families, and their communities. But Buwei Yang Chao's Chinese cooking found an audience that went far beyond her own family.

Buwei didn't start out as a cook. Born in China, she first immigrated to Japan to study medicine but was dissatisfied with the food and began learning to cook the dishes of her homeland. After returning to China, she earned a degree in gynecology and was one of the first female practitioners of Western medicine in the country.

Later, she relocated again—this time to Massachusetts, where she often cooked for her husband and his colleagues. The guests at her table surprised her with their enthusiasm for her food and encouraged her to write a Chinese cookbook. Buwei wasn't comfortable writing in English, so her daughter and husband helped her pen *How to Cook and Eat in Chinese*—the book in which "stir-fry" and "pot sticker" got their English names. The book was published in 1945 and, in addition to recipes, included helpful cultural cues for first-time Chinese diners, even diagrams showing how to hold chopsticks. Buwei later wrote a second book, *How to Order and Eat in Chinese to Get the Best Meal in a Chinese Restaurant*, as well as an autobiography.

Cristeta Comerford

1962 - PRESENT

AS THE FIRST WOMAN and nonwhite person to hold the title of White House executive chef, Cristeta Comerford knows a thing or two about working under pressure. She caters functions for official state guests, plans and executes menus for elaborate banquets and receptions, and, to top it all off, feeds the president and the first family every day.

Possessed of remarkable culinary prowess and a collaborative temperament, Cristeta has worked in the White House kitchen for more than twenty years, spanning the tenure of four presidents: Bill Clinton, George W. Bush, Barack Obama, and Donald J. Trump. When it comes to hiring the White House executive chef, the first lady wields the power, but everyone in the White House serves at the pleasure of the president. Cristeta's first job

in the White House was as sous chef under Hillary Clinton, and she rose to executive chef in 2005 under Laura Bush. Her flawless execution of an official state dinner for Indian prime minister Manmohan Singh and 134 guests so impressed Mrs. Bush that she put her in charge of the entire White House kitchen.

Cristeta was born in the Philippines. In 1985, she moved with her family from Manila to Chicago, where she became a cook, rising through the ranks from salad chef at hotel restaurants to *chef tournant*—a Jill-of-all-trades cook equipped to handle every station in a professional kitchen. She later honed her knowledge in Vienna, mastering classic French techniques.

Over her many-decade career, Cristeta has proven that the heat of the kitchen is no match for her cool and steady focus. On the front lines of dinner diplomacy, she creates menus that incorporate the influences of visiting nations while showcasing the best of American cuisine. She is a representative for the United States on a global stage, and a powerful leader for women everywhere.

Marie Harel

1761-1844

AMONG THE CREAMY, STINKY, sweet, salty, and sometimes moldy varieties that occupy the top echelon of French cheesedom, there is one that won over World War II troops and became a symbol of French identity: the beloved Camembert. The woman who created it, Marie Harel, has earned an equal amount of fame and devotion.

The legend of this famous cheese takes us to Normandy at the turn of the eighteenth century, amid the tumult of the French Revolution. Somewhere near the village of Camembert, a local cheesemaker sheltered a priest

on the run from an angry mob. The clergyman, himself a cheesemaker from Brie, passed his knowledge on to the woman, Marie. The result of their collaboration? An aromatic cheese called Camembert.

It's a lovely legend, but here's a more likely version. Born in Crouttes on April 28, 1761, Marie worked on her family's farm in Camembert, where she produced cheese according to local custom. Her skill with the creamy cheese was so superlative that her variety became synonymous with the Camembert style, and she later passed her craft on to her daughter and son-in-law, who kicked off a new era of the family business. All of Marie's five grandchildren also became cheesemakers, expanding the production of Camembert and ensuring that the cheese found fans far beyond its birthplace.

Today, Camembert falls into the category of *les fromages à pâte molle et à croûte fleurie*—that's the fancy French way of saying "soft cheeses with a natural rind." There are plenty of imitators, but the real deal is specifically labeled as Camembert de Normandie A.O.C. Raw Normande cow's milk is inoculated with bacteria, rennet, and the *Penicillium camemberti* mold that gives Camembert its iconic soft white rind. After the cheese has ripened, *fromage* fans can enjoy its rich, creamy texture solo, served at room temperature to allow the complex flavors to bloom, baked and paired with fruits and nuts, or even inside gooey homemade mac and cheese. Regardless of how Marie found her calling in the creation of Camembert, *that's* the stuff of legend.

BAKED CAMEMBERT

SERVES 4

This is a quick and easy customizable cheese course that pairs perfectly with a variety of options.

EQUIPMENT: Camembert wooden box or small ceramic baking dish

1 (8- or 9-ounce) wheel of Camembert in wooden box

1–2 garlic cloves, sliced into matchsticks

2 sprigs fresh thyme, stems removed

Cracked black pepper

Honey

Preheat oven to 350°F.

Remove and discard wrapper from Camembert and place cheese back in wooden box (if your Camembert did not come with wooden box, place cheese inside ceramic baking dish). Score top rind of cheese with knife in crosshatch pattern and insert garlic into cheese. Sprinkle top with thyme and cracked black pepper, and drizzle with honey. Bake Camembert for 15–20 minutes until gooey. Be careful not to overbake, or cheese will dry out and harden.

Remove from oven and serve immediately with crackers, fruit and herb crisps, toasted slices of baguette, walnuts, dried fruit, or whatever suits your fancy.

Julia Child

1912-2004

THROUGH HER EXPERTISE and sense of humor, Julia Child introduced French cooking to America, freeing home cooks from the drudgery of canned-soup casseroles and TV dinners. One of the first cooks to demonstrate techniques on live TV, she possessed a larger-than-life personality that she poured into living rooms and kitchens. Julia encouraged home cooks to abandon fears of kitchen failure and take pleasure in a job well done.

Culinary success came later in life for Julia. Her path toward food emerged while she was working for the U.S. government in the Office of Strategic Services, where she met the love of her life, diplomat Paul Child. Paul's assignment took the couple to Paris, where Julia became hooked on *la cuisine française*.

Midcentury home cooking was a woman's domain, where efficiency often outweighed ingenuity—and flavor. But professional kitchens, those havens of culinary creativity, were ruled by men. Fortunately for us, Julia paid no mind. She enrolled in the legendary cooking school Le Cordon Bleu. The only woman in a cooking class for aspiring professionals, Julia excelled despite the school's efforts to keep her from graduating. She found kindred spirits in two fellow students, Simone Beck and Louisette Bertholle, and together they launched their own cooking school, L'École des Trois Gourmandes (School of the Three Happy Eaters). It was geared toward American expat housewives, and Julia's teaching experience helped her write her magnum opus, the first English cookbook on French cuisine for Americans.

The philosophy of American cooking in the 1950s focused on one thing: convenience. During the industrial food revolution, mass-produced, highly preserved foods—initially rations for World War II troops—were marketed as quick and easy go-tos for American households. Meals made from boxes and cans, instant mashed potatoes, soups, Spam, and TV dinners were "foods of the future." But then, like a breath of fresh air, came *Mastering the Art of French Cooking*. A behemoth—nearly seven hundred pages—emboldened homemakers to venture outside their comfort zone to cook the French way. Most books of the day favored easy mealtime solutions, but Julia's book required the reader to pay careful attention to techniques and to the quality of fresh ingredients. In exchange, her clear instructions helped cooks conquer the challenges of foreign cuisine.

In the 1960s, Julia's influential TV show, *The French Chef*, debuted. The charming, charismatic, and at times hilarious six-foot-two chef whipped up her recipes, giving home cooks the confidence to follow suit. She owned her gaffes, gleefully dropping the French slang *Je m'en foutisme* ("I don't care") in response to an unintentionally airborne spatula or the premature unmolding of a loose tarte tatin. Julia knew the significance of hosting and sharing a meal, and never let something like a messy omelet interfere with the courage, the pride, or the pure joy of cooking.

Marjorie Husted
~&~
Betty Crocker

1892-1986

BEFORE SHE BECAME SYNONYMOUS with red boxes of fudgy brownie and birthday cake mixes, Betty Crocker was merely a figment of the imagination. And while she never actually lived, in the determined, capable hands of Marjorie Husted, Betty became a cultural icon and a very real inspiration for nearly a century of women.

Marjorie graduated from the University of Minnesota in 1913. She worked for the Red Cross during World War I, and later at the Women's Cooperative Alliance, in Minneapolis, before taking a job in 1924 as a home economist at the Minnesota firm Washburn-Crosby, the brand that would become General Mills. Three years earlier, the company had introduced a character called Betty Crocker. She was the invention of an advertising department composed of men—men who were completely unprepared for the enthusiastic response to the figure they'd created. The company was

inundated with letters from women inquiring about perfecting their piecrust or maintaining moisture in their home-baked cakes, so an all-female staff was organized to answer each letter as Betty herself. In 1929, Marjorie took over that department, then known as the Betty Crocker Homemaking Service. She saw an opportunity to promote the personality and brand—and to meet the needs of homemakers, who she felt could use a little support, even if it did come from a fictional character.

Under her supervision, Betty would go on to have her own radio show (with Marjorie herself occasionally voicing the character), a television program, a cookbook, and a line of pantry products, including the famous cake mixes.

The character became a major part of the General Mills brand and the company's success, thanks largely to Marjorie's work. She was awarded Advertising Woman of the Year in 1949 and also served as a consultant to the U.S. Department of Agriculture.

Betty's iconic signature has become synonymous with housewives in quaint home kitchens, but in fact, Betty herself was quite a feminine force. Even early on, she was never depicted as having children or a husband to answer to but instead presented as a confident, independent authority figure. A feminist and firebrand, Marjorie sensed the importance of this kind of leader for the female community. In an interview with *Twin Cities Magazine*, she said of the nation's women, "Here were millions of them staying at home alone, doing a job with children, cooking, cleaning on minimal budgets—the whole depressing mess of it. They needed someone to remind them they had value." Betty Crocker has given millions of cake lovers a little bit of joy with her advice and her treats, and has also shown women around the country and the world not only how to keep their homes, but what they're worth.

M.F.K. Fisher

1908 – 1992

I T'S PRETTY SAFE TO say that without M.F.K. Fisher, the O.G. (that's "original gastronome"), this book might not be in your hands. During Mary Frances Kennedy Fisher's life, which spanned nearly the entire twentieth century, many women were finding their culinary voices (just take a look through these pages for evidence). All around her, new cookbooks recorded culinary traditions and offered education and recipes for home cooks. But Mary became one of the most influential voices in culinary writing while publishing barely any recipes.

She was married several times, and if the abundance of locales in which she lived—sunny Los Angeles, the French countryside, Switzerland, New York City, and Northern California—are any indication, Mary was a romantic with a serious case of wanderlust. It's hardly a surprise, given that she was writing poetry by age five. She was born into a family of food and word lovers. Her father tried his hand at farming with the purchase of an orange grove in Southern California and later owned a small newspaper where Mary cut her teeth. She also spent her early years helping her mother in the kitchen and always adored the work.

In her adventures across continents, dropping in and out of different worlds, Mary absorbed it all, the food, the culture, the people. She was a natural scribe and observer, and by the time she started writing about food, she had an expansive collection of experiences to draw from. For Mary, food wasn't just about cooking—it was about *life*. She accessed themes and emotions common to all readers, using food as the connecting thread. She wrote coming-of-age stories. She wrote about grief and death—as in *An Alphabet for Gourmets*, when she committed to paper the words "S is for sad...and for the mysterious appetite that often surges in us when our hearts seem about to break and our lives too bleakly empty." She wrote about love and lust and relationships—her own romantic ones and the ones she had with what she ate. She even wrote about war, in *How to Cook a Wolf*, a book that addresses the practicalities of eating during economic and political turmoil. In a style that presaged the modern-day food memoir, her stories were personal, and by using food as an access point for so many ubiquitous feelings, she demonstrated the relationship between human sensuality and eating with all the senses. And like all great art, hers was provocative. Mary's writings so deftly blended the epicurean and the experiential that she made some contemporary readers uncomfortable, and she was not critically embraced while she lived. But to her, food was the perfect vehicle for human emotion. Of her writing, Mary herself said, "It seems to me that our three basic needs, for food and security and love, are so mixed and mingled and entwined that we cannot straightly think of one without the others."

She wrote more than thirty books over her six-decade career, not to mention hundreds of essays and contributions to magazines like *The New Yorker, Vogue,* and *Town and Country*—plus a few novels for good measure. One of her most well-known contributions to the culinary bookshelf is her translation of Jean Anthelme Brillat-Savarin's *Physiology of Taste*, considered the first-ever work of food writing.

Today, Mary might be astonished at the number of people who make a career writing food memoirs, essays, and even fiction. In her obituary, the *New York Times* observed that she was a "writer whose artful personal essays about food created a genre." By writing what she felt and always following her heart, and the food, she stimulated readers' appetites for a new kind of writing, poignant and playful and not purely instructional. She prepared the world for future generations to pick up where she left off, and she let us know that food—not just eating it, but reading and writing about it—can be about pleasure, about joy, and about love.

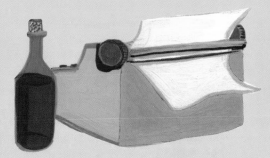

Madhur Jaffrey

1933 - PRESENT

MADHUR JAFFREY may have started her career as an actress, but it was her performance in the kitchen that defined her as the leading lady of Indian cuisine.

With roots running back through the British Raj into the Mughal Empire, Madhur was born into privilege and grew up in Delhi under British colonialism. Since household servants handled all domestic chores, including cooking, she was never taught the workings of a kitchen. But as a college student at the Royal Academy of Dramatic Art in London, when faced with the

gray meat and tortured vegetables of the school canteen, Madhur knew she had to call for backup. Her mother became her lifeline, airmailing simple recipes designed to teach the basics of Indian cuisine: cauliflower and potatoes, roasted eggplant, and uncomplicated meat dishes.

Madhur moved to New York to pursue her acting career, but being an Indian actress in America, she found herself with limited roles—and more time in the kitchen. She began hosting dinner parties for curious Americans, her rebuke to local Indian restaurants' inauthentic and unimaginative offerings. Later, as wife and mother of three daughters, she fell into food writing for magazines and newspapers to supplement her family's income. After winning best actress at the Berlin International Film Festival for her breakthrough role in 1965's *Shakespeare Wallah,* Madhur was approached by *New York Times* food writer Craig Claiborne for an article on her connection with Indian cuisine. The piece put her in the spotlight not for her acting ability, but her cooking.

Madhur was frustrated with the oversimplified representation of Indian food. She vehemently opposed the ubiquity of the word "curry" in describing a vast array of flavors and was inspired to put her recipes on paper. In 1973, she published *An Invitation to Indian Cooking,* the first Indian cookbook for an American audience. In 2006, her book received a place in the James Beard Foundation Cookbook Hall of Fame. Following its success, Madhur once again found herself in front of the camera, this time on the small screen. In 1982, the BBC approached her for an educational cooking show centered on Indian cuisine, and the result was *Madhur Jaffrey's Indian Cookery,* which quickly crossed over to America on PBS.

In her many popular cookbooks and on television, Madhur encouraged Western cooks to invite Indian cuisine into their kitchens. She found her calling in guiding the curious through the unique regions of her home, a journey that took them halfway around the world.

MASALA SALMON

SERVES 4 TO 6

EQUIPMENT: Sheet pan, tinfoil

1 tablespoon olive oil

2 pounds salmon fillets, skin on

1 teaspoon sesame oil

1 teaspoon kosher salt

1 teaspoon cracked black pepper

2 teaspoons garlic, minced

1 teaspoon mirin

1½ teaspoons ginger paste

6–8 capers

½ teaspoon soy sauce

¼ teaspoon mustard powder

¼ teaspoon rosemary, crushed in palm of hand

½ teaspoon crushed red pepper

1 teaspoon tandoori masala

1 lemon, halved

Preheat oven to 390°F.

Line sheet pan with tinfoil and grease with olive oil. Rinse salmon, pat dry, and place skin side down on tinfoil. Lightly rub sesame oil over entire surface of fish. Season with salt and cracked black pepper. Pat minced garlic evenly onto salmon. Sprinkle mirin across surface. With spoon, spread ginger paste from corner to corner. Place capers across surface of fish. Drizzle with soy sauce. Sprinkle mustard powder, rosemary, and crushed red pepper over salmon. Finish with even sprinkling of tandoori masala. Place salmon in oven and bake for 22 minutes or until flesh is opaque and flaky, rotating pan midway through baking and squeezing lemon over salmon. Once salmon is done, remove pan from oven and squeeze lemon over fish again. Cover with tinfoil and let sit for 10 minutes before serving.

Serve salmon on bed of basmati rice or vegetable pilaf.

NOTE *Masala is a traditional Indian mixture of spices that play off one another. Be sure to evenly distribute all ingredients across the entire surface of the salmon.*

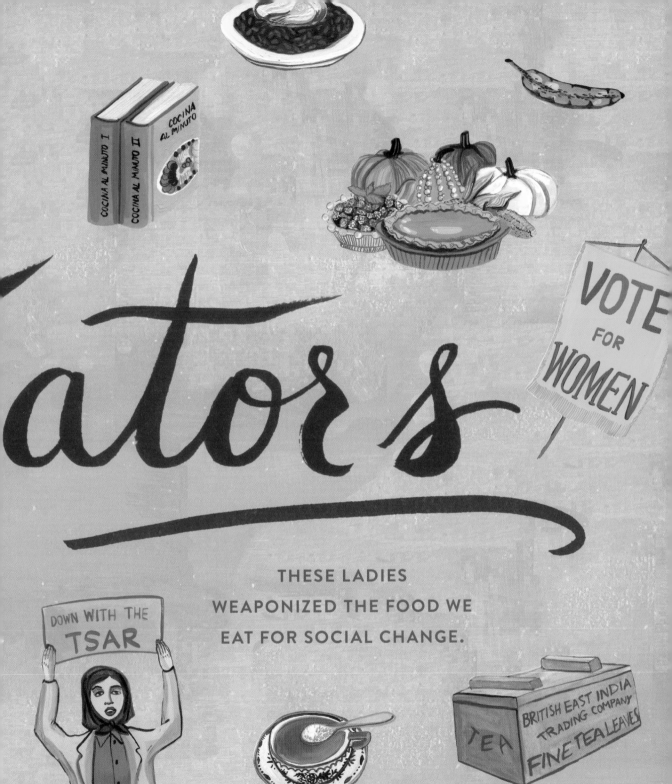

ators

THESE LADIES
WEAPONIZED THE FOOD WE
EAT FOR SOCIAL CHANGE.

Women of Protest

EIGHTEENTH AND TWENTIETH CENTURIES

THE WOMEN OF VERSAILLES While King Louis XVI and Marie Antoinette were busy having a ball in their palace at Versailles, French commoners were desperately struggling for food. A roller coaster of adverse weather events—drought, flooding, and severe frost—pummeled crops and produced poor harvests. Bread became so scarce, and consequently so expensive, that Parisian workers were spending up to 90 percent of their hard-earned dough on bread. In October 1789, nearly seven thousand angry musket- and pitchfork-wielding women gathered in Paris, ready to riot. They marched the twelve miles to Versailles, picking up more incensed ladies along the way.

Instigators

They arrived at the palace chanting for bread and the next day escorted the royal family back to Paris to meet a revolutionary force—and, a few years later, their deaths.

THE WOMEN OF THE RUSSIAN REVOLUTION When the men of Russia went off to the First World War, nearly a million women—many of whom had never worked outside the home—filled the jobs they left behind. But their wages were half those of their male counterparts, and long hours in factories followed by long lines for bread inflamed their anger. On March 8, 1917—International Women's Day—after the government announced food rationing, frustrated women took to the streets in droves to demand bread for the workers. Numbers swelled as more women, and some inspired men, joined the revolt, and the Duma, the Russian assembly, was incapacitated by the daily demonstrations. With Tsar Nicholas II stationed at a military base four hundred miles away, the Romanov dynasty's grip crumbled as even its own soldiers joined the protest. By the time the tsar reached home shortly thereafter, his reign was virtually over; he abdicated on March 15.

KAMALADEVI CHATTOPADHYAY AND THE WOMEN OF THE SALT PROTEST AT CHOWPATTY BEACH An attack on salt is an attack on every cook. With the India Salt Act of 1882, the British colonial government in India forced Indian families to import expensive salt from it. This meant huge profits for the East India Company and the crown, but it was the last straw for a nation already yearning for self-governance. Independence movement leader Mohandas Gandhi and his followers launched a nonviolent protest against British rule, the Salt Satyagraha (a term coined by Gandhi for passive resistance, literally "holding on to truth"). In 1930, freedom fighter and loyal Gandhi supporter Kamaladevi Chattopadhyay caught wind of the salt march and formed a group of her own. She and her female followers joined Gandhi in the nearly 250-mile march to coastal Chowpatty, with makeshift

stoves, or *chulhas*, in hand. They set up shop on the beach and boiled seawater to extract their own salt. When police raided the site with batons swinging, Kamaladevi was struck. She fell into live coals but, despite severe burns, refused to leave the protest to receive treatment. Her bravery inspired more women to join, and their salt was auctioned in Bombay in defiance of the law. For days, women protested; they vandalized the Congress building by creating salt pans on the terrace and, when the police tried to shut down their protests, formed human shields to block the path. Kamaladevi wasn't done just yet. She led a march five hundred strong on April 16 to Wadala Salt Depot, where they collected the natural salt and sold it. Kamaladevi was scheduled to lead another march to the salt depot a month later but was arrested two days before that second demonstration. Still, more than two thousand people marched there without her. Salt—one of the world's most ubiquitous and critical commodities—became a powerful, unifying symbol in India's revolt against British colonialism. The Salt Satyagraha, and its fearless commando, Kamaladevi, were the beginning of India's fight for independence, with some extraordinary women at its front line.

Georgia Gilmore

1920-1990

GEORGIA GILMORE IS PROOF that making a difference doesn't require a spotlight—just a stovetop and an oven. Georgia was an activist during the civil rights movement who used food to finance the Montgomery bus boycott, a turning point in America's fight for racial equality.

After Rosa Parks refused to relinquish her seat to a white passenger on a segregated bus, her arrest sparked a widespread bus boycott in the city of Montgomery, Alabama. Spearheaded by a young Reverend Martin Luther King, Jr., it was the first large-scale protest against segregation in U.S. history. Rosa Parks and Martin Luther King, Jr., are names now known the world over—but it was Georgia who fed the movement. Inspired by Rosa's simple protest, she started selling chicken sandwiches at protest meetings, though

she knew she could raise even more money with some help from her community. She formed the Club from Nowhere (cleverly named so women could remain honest about their cash source—it came "from nowhere"), recruiting other women to roll up their sleeves and cook. In laundromats, beauty salons, and churches all over Montgomery, they sold everything from chicken and pork chops to pound cakes and sweet potato pies. More than six hundred dollars raised every week paid for African Americans to get to work without having to rely on the bus system, helping to reinforce the boycott.

When King and fellow leaders were indicted for unlawful conspiracy, Georgia fearlessly testified at the trial, speaking out against a white bus driver who had kicked her off his bus. She was consequently fired from her job, but that didn't keep her down. With King's support, she started her own restaurant and frequently hosted King and other prominent leaders, including Robert F. Kennedy and Lyndon B. Johnson.

The peaceful protest, made possible with cash from the Club from Nowhere, punished the Montgomery bus system. Ultimately, the U.S. Supreme Court intervened. Citing a violation of the Fourteenth Amendment, the highest court in the land ordered the integration of local buses. After 381 days, the boycott was over.

Georgia gave black women—workers, maids, and housewives—a way of supporting the civil rights movement without fear of retaliation from white employers and landlords. By using abilities each woman already possessed, she and the ladies of Montgomery helped steer the course of American history.

The Haenyeo

SEVENTEENTH CENTURY— PRESENT

ON THE KOREAN ISLAND of Jeju, a society of women balances on the edge of life and death. For over four hundred years, they've plunged to depths of nearly forty feet without breathing equipment to pluck treasures from the sea. This free-diving tribe of fearless women known as *haenyeo*—literally, "sea women"—challenged the patriarchal norms of mainland Korea. There, women were expected to be subordinate and economically dependent on men. But as the primary breadwinners on the island, these women have formed a sisterhood that is a symbol of female independence and strength.

Like that of so many food pioneers, the story of the haenyeo is one of necessity. In the seventeenth century, many of Jeju's men went to sea, either for work or for war. The responsibility of diving for abalone—once a man's job—fell to the women. Fearful of retribution if they failed to deliver, they

shouldered the burden to keep pace with demand from Korea's elite. The haenyeo performed perilous work diligently and regardless of circumstance, at times even while pregnant. Today, their tradition continues, and after centuries, their abalone, sea urchin, clams, octopus, seaweed, and other edible jewels feed more than royalty; they are a major part of the island's economy.

With nothing more than a mask, a pair of flippers, and a weight belt, the haenyeo dive into the frigid waters of the Jeju Strait. Exhausting dives lasting up to seven hours per day can prove fatal. While testing their human limits, the haenyeo rely on the divine for support, saying a prayer—or *jamsu-gut*—to the sea gods before each mission.

Beyond being badasses of the high seas, the haenyeo were also pioneers of sustainable fishing practices. Even today, they use no modern machinery, to prevent overfishing. Instead, with either a spear or bare hands, the ladies comb the seafloor for as long as they can hold their breath.

The knowledge of the haenyeo is passed from mother to daughter, but there are warning signs of the custom's extinction. The average age of haenyeo is over fifty; the eldest member is over ninety. Most young women from Jeju are choosing different career paths, opting out of the hard life of free diving. With numbers diminishing from over fourteen thousand in the 1970s to a little over four thousand today, a new fear among these sea women is not of their own death, but that of their culture.

Fortunately, the South Korean government is working to preserve their heritage: a haenyeo museum has been established to encourage cultural awareness, and it now subsidizes health insurance for all haenyeo. And with the addition of the haenyeo to the 2016 UNESCO Intangible Cultural Heritage list, there is hope their work will live on and inspire a new generation of diving women.

The haenyeo created a system of economics and society based on female power. For these resilient women, dignity comes from hard work, a centuries-old, unbreakable bond with nature, and with one another.

Women in Convents

TWELFTH CENTURY– PRESENT

ORA ET LABORA. **PRAY AND LABOR.** For centuries, nuns lived pious and humble lives following exactly this Benedictine principle. But behind the walls of their cloisters, they quietly produced delicious sweets and baked goods, creating heavenly delicacies while always in service of the Heavenly Father. They often sold their labor-intensive treats through a "wheel"—a revolving hatch where coins disappeared and pastries magically materialized. As far back as the twelfth century, sweets were a source of income for convents, and their tidbits became free advertising. Even today, nuns sell breads, honey, and jams to the public, keeping with tradition in order to preserve it.

Instigators

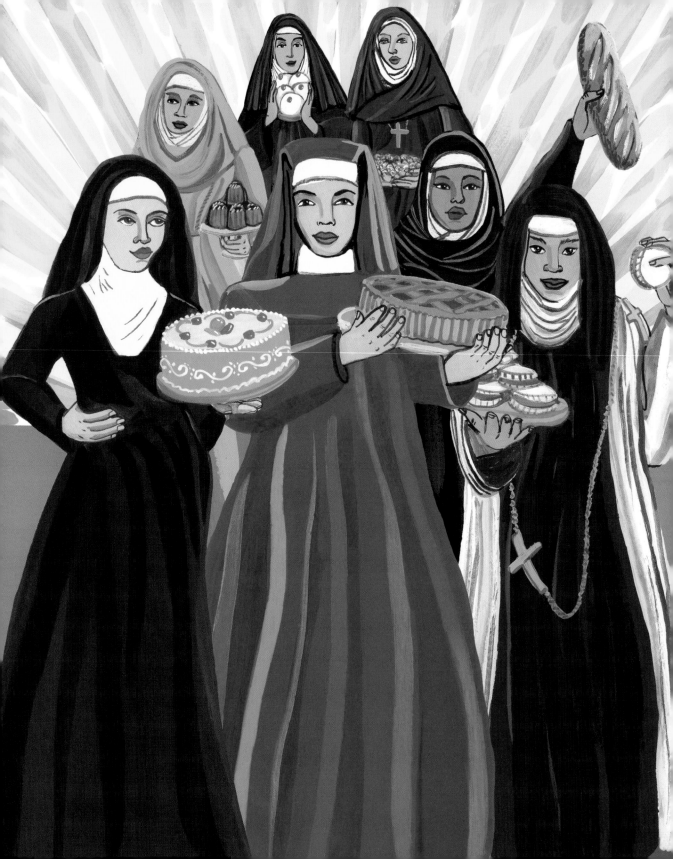

SOR JUANA INÉS DE LA CRUZ Sor Juana Inés de la Cruz, a seventeenth-century nun of the San Jerónimo Monastery in Mexico City, wrote a small book on convent life that provides powerful insight into colonial Mexico's culinary heritage.

The daughter of a Spaniard and a criolla woman, Sor Juana had an uncanny intellect and a wild sense of curiosity. The convent kitchen became her laboratory, where she tinkered with ingredients and observed their transformations. The majority of Sor Juana's recipes focus on desserts, most likely because sweets were an important source of income. They represent a range of dishes that still make up the Mexican canon, like *mamey sapote*, *alfajores*, and *cajeta*.

For historians, understanding the inner workings of a convent has long been a challenge due to the guarded nature of the nuns within. Sor Juana's recipes preserved gastronomic heritage, and served as a looking glass into convent life. In *La Respuesta a Sor Filotea de la Cruz*, Sor Juana's brilliant response to a priest who tried to silence her, she uses food and cooking as metaphors for learning, female intellect, and women's right to education, making the case that the kitchen was not only a place for nourishment, but enlightenment as well.

MARIA GRAMMATICO Considered the authority on Sicilian pastries, Maria Grammatico wasn't a nun, but she was raised by them. After World War II, poverty afflicted many parts of Europe, and Sicily was no exception. After the death of her father left her family destitute, eleven-year-old Maria and her sister were placed by their mother in the care of the convent and orphanage of San Carlo in Erice.

Maria worked in the cloister and learned to make Sicilian desserts. Her young hands shelled almonds and fashioned the apricots, pears, apples, and pomegranates of *frutta martorana* (marzipan fruits). She learned to make almond and other pastries (*genovesi*, *sospiri*, and *palline*) as well as jam and cream tarts. Convent life was hard and lean, but for fifteen years, Maria honed the skills that would one day make her one of the most respected *pasticcieri* in Sicily.

She eventually opened a humble pastry shop in Erice. Through sheer determination, she made a name for herself and, ultimately, for the town, where droves of sweet-toothed tourists and locals still descend on her little shop. Through her eponymous cooking school, Maria continues to preserve centuries-old recipes, passing on her own rich education to future generations.

Hattie Burr and the Suffragettes

1880s - 1920

"THIS LITTLE BOOK IS sent out with an important mission." Perhaps a lofty introduction for a cookbook. But the one edited and compiled by Boston-born Hattie Burr was unlike anything a home cook had seen before. Hattie's readers didn't pick up her book in search of Sunday night dinner ideas—though they found those in its pages, too. This book had a recipe for revolution.

Before the ratification of the Nineteenth Amendment, in 1920, when decisions about who would run our country rested entirely in the hands of men, a group of women committed to making a woman's right to vote a reality. They were scrappy and creative, and knew that the only way to succeed was by leveraging the skills they shared. In the late nineteenth century, women weren't considered capable of or fit for any sort of formal financial responsibility. But they were expected to run a household, cook, clean, preside over household staff (if they were women of means), and take charge of charities and other philanthropic efforts. Men felt this was women's work. What those men didn't expect was that this work taught women to organize, raise money, manage teams, and collaborate—all the skills they'd need to fight for their freedom.

It was a good thing, because when the time came to win the vote, the fight for suffrage was costly. Cash was needed to print materials, to organize demonstrations, marches, and rallies, even parades and transcontinental trips, and the suffragettes were forced to find innovative ways to raise funds. Bake sales had already proven a useful way to convert their prowess in the kitchen to financial gain. The next step was obvious: publish a cookbook.

The Woman Suffrage Cook Book, published in November 1886 with Hattie at the helm, had contributors that read like a *Who's Who* of accomplished American women. Over the next two decades, more than half a dozen such recipe collections would be published in support of female suffrage, with contributions from the likes of journalist Mary Livermore, poet Julia Ward Howe, abolitionist Abby Kelley, newspaper editor Abigail Scott Duniway, physician and minister Anna Howard Shaw, novelist Charlotte Perkins Gilman, and many other remarkable women.

But the books were far more than a fund-raising device. Through them, suffragettes could communicate across distances and demonstrate support. Call it a turn-of-the-century Twitter. In fact, the cookbooks were more like

Trojan horses, spreading a radical agenda under the guise of simple recipes. They gave practical instructions for the respectable housewife—like how to feed a crowd—but they also allowed women to tease their opponents and commiserate about their struggle. One book featured a Pie for a Suffragist's Doubting Husband, with ingredients such as "1 qt milk of human kindness." Others called for "1 lb Truth, thoroughly mangled" and "1 generous handful of injustice" in recipes designed to stoke women's frustration over being second-class citizens, with each wink and nod. With practical exercises, like a recipe for Election Cake, a treat to be distributed at the polls as a voting incentive, the books had a call to action baked right in.

The cookbooks served a culinary purpose, but also delivered a powerful warning: *don't underestimate us*. In them, the suffragettes united their collective strengths and voices, drawing on what they knew—what was already expected of them—and using it as a tool to strike at domestic oppression. Today, the fiery resolve of these women lives on in Hattie's preface of November 25, 1886: "I believe the great value of these contributions will be fully appreciated, and our messenger will go forth...an advocate for the elevation and enfranchisement of women."

NUTMEG ELECTION CAKE WITH MAPLE CREAM CHEESE FROSTING

SERVES 16 TO 20

The suffragettes' Election Cake was a simple nutmeg loaf cake.
Try this delicious treat for your next bake sale or community event.

EQUIPMENT: 9 x 13-inch pan, stand or hand mixer

NUTMEG ELECTION CAKE
3 cups cake flour, sifted

1½ cups light brown sugar

2¼ teaspoons baking powder

1 teaspoon ground nutmeg

¾ teaspoon baking soda

¾ teaspoon kosher salt

½ teaspoon ground cinnamon

2 cups buttermilk, room temperature

2 large eggs, room temperature

1 large egg yolk, room temperature

4½ tablespoons unsalted butter, melted, room temperature

MAPLE CREAM CHEESE FROSTING
1½ cups confectioners' sugar, sifted

1 (8-ounce) package cream cheese, room temperature

1 stick (½ cup) unsalted butter, room temperature

½ teaspoon ground nutmeg

½ teaspoon kosher salt

½ cup Grade A dark pure maple syrup

Make the Nutmeg Election Cake: Preheat oven to 350°F.

To measure flour, use spoon to fill measuring cup loosely and then level with knife.

Combine all dry ingredients in mixing bowl. In separate bowl, whisk all wet ingredients together, then add to dry mixture. Using spatula, begin gently folding ingredients together until batter is combined and no dry ingredients

· *RECIPE CONTINUES* ·

are visible. Be careful not to overmix, as this will cause excess gluten to form. Transfer batter to greased pan, tapping pan on countertop to level batter. Bake immediately for 28–30 minutes or until golden brown and toothpick inserted in center comes out clean. Cake will have a slightly domed top, spring back when touched, and begin to pull away from edges of pan when done.

Let cool for 10 minutes in pan, then invert onto wire rack to finish cooling. Once cake is completely cooled, invert onto serving platter before frosting.

Make the Maple Cream Cheese Frosting: To measure confectioners' sugar, use spoon to fill measuring cup loosely and then level with knife. Using stand mixer with paddle attachment or hand mixer, beat together sugar, cream cheese, butter, nutmeg, and salt until smooth. Add maple syrup and mix until thoroughly combined. Using offset spatula, spread ¼- to ½-inch-thick layer of frosting on cooled cake.

Mary Seacole

1805–1881

IN THE NINETEENTH CENTURY, traveling the world wasn't part of the lifestyle of the average woman, let alone a woman of mixed race. But Mary Seacole was far from average. She was a lifelong globe-trotter, entrepreneur, and one of her generation's most active humanitarians.

Mary was born in Jamaica at the turn of the nineteenth century, the daughter of a Scottish soldier. But it was her free black Jamaican mother—a traditional healer who operated a boardinghouse in Kingston—who set Mary on her path as a nurse and caretaker. During her youth, she learned healing techniques, both at her mother's hand and from the military doctors who boarded with them. Early in life, Mary caught the travel bug; in her

autobiography, she wrote about adventures in California, Panama, England, and beyond. Her experiences made her uniquely worldly and aware, and inspired in her an empathy that no doubt informed her later humanitarian efforts. Her journeys were also entrepreneurial; after traveling to Haiti, Cuba, the Bahamas, and elsewhere, Mary became an importer, sourcing and collecting spices and preserves to sell back in Jamaica. After she contracted cholera during an epidemic in the 1850s, she traveled to Panama upon her recovery and used her knowledge to treat others. There she also opened a canteen to feed the locals and to trade food, wine, and medicine.

When she learned of the Crimean War, Mary again felt compelled to react to a global crisis. She traveled to the London War Office to offer her services but was turned away because of the color of her skin. Mary refused to take no for an answer. In the mid-1850s, at her own expense, she sailed to the Crimea to support soldiers in need. At her boardinghouse near the front lines, she independently nursed and fed soldiers, who appreciated her stews, curries, custards, pastries, and rice puddings so much, they gave her the nickname Mother Seacole.

Mary would have been an unusually brave and caring soul in any era, but today, when we can hardly imagine bipartisanship in a single nation, her profound empathy, which extended beyond borders, seems especially remarkable. Even though she suffered personal discrimination, she saw no dividing line; she treated the wounded on either side of a conflict without question. In the later years of her life, Mary returned to London in poor health and with very little money. But in 1857, more than eighty thousand attended a fundraiser in her honor, and British royalty—encouraged by appreciative officers of the war—established a fund to support her for the rest of her life. During that time, Mary turned her adventures into an autobiographical travelogue, the first of its kind to be published in England by a black woman. *Wonderful Adventures of Mrs. Seacole in Many Lands* became a bestseller.

Lady Eve Balfour

1898–1990

FOR EVERY ORGANIC BERRY breakfast parfait, farm-focused restaurant menu, and "health food" itself, we have Lady Eve Balfour to thank. Before it became a global food trend, the word "organic" referred to holistic farming and its direct effect on our food and bodies. Eve authored the classic study of soil science and biology, *The Living Soil*, which made a case for organic farming as healthier not just for the soil, but for the food grown in it—and generated awareness for an international movement.

From a young age, Eve knew farming was her calling. Born in England in 1898 into an aristocratic and politically active family, she was one of the first women permitted to study agriculture and wasted no time putting her education to use. At age twenty-one, she and her sister purchased New Bells Farm in Suffolk. The land became Eve's lab.

She was a founding member of the Soil Association, formed in 1946 as a response to intensive farming—the government-approved effort to ramp up food production through the use of chemical fertilizers and pesticides as an answer to post–World War II food rationing. She conducted a study of different farming methods and their impact on the health of the soil, as well as of the nutritional value of the food grown there. Eve and her team used these insights to formulate the first practical standards for organic farming. Today, the association is responsible for certifying 70 percent of organic food in the United Kingdom.

Through the 1950s, Eve traveled extensively to spread her organic gospel, from North America to Australia, New Zealand, and parts of Europe. She helped found IFOAM, the International Federation of Organic Agriculture Movements. She believed in growing and eating local, demanding strict regulations on land used for food production to promote the safety and health of those who ate from it. In farmers markets and grocery stores, from fancy restaurant menus to modern street fare, Eve's philosophy of healthful farming lives on in our food choices today.

Beatrice de Luna

1510–1569

THE SPICE ROUTES OF the sixteenth century presented a whole new world of culinary exploration and experimentation. Exotic powders, seeds, roots, and barks were introduced to the West and were used for flavor, medicine, currency, and even as a preservative for perishable foods. But for one woman who led this new global trade, spices provided a road for something else worth saving—hundreds of human lives.

Beatrice de Luna was born in the early 1500s in Portugal and later married Francisco Mendes, a wealthy trader whose company specialized in Portuguese peppers and spices. Both were crypto-Jews—forced to practice

their true faith in secret, while acting as Christians in public. But Francisco died young, and he left Beatrice with an infant just as Pope Paul III launched the Portuguese Inquisition.

Beatrice and her daughter fled to Antwerp, where Francisco's brother was operating a branch of the family trading empire. There she took a larger role and began developing her own side of the business. Well supported by the profits from this enterprise, Beatrice recognized an opportunity to help *conversos*—Jewish converts to Christianity under the Inquisition. She organized and financed the escape from Portugal of hundreds of Jews aboard her spice-trading ships. Once they arrived in Antwerp, she supplied the refugees with funds and resources to travel to the Ottoman Empire, where Jews were free to practice their religion openly.

Beatrice went on to live in Italy and ultimately settled in Istanbul, where she financed settlements for refugees and infrastructure for the Jewish community. She also used her fortune to translate Hebrew texts into Spanish—all while repeatedly dodging governments that continuously sought to relieve her of her fortune because of her religious affiliation.

Until her death, in 1569, Beatrice advocated for her people because she knew that while new ingredients could make the food they enjoyed more exciting, it was community that gave life its real spice.

School Lunch Leaders

LATE NINETEENTH AND EARLY TWENTIETH CENTURIES

A T THE TURN OF THE TWENTIETH CENTURY, the economic inequality facing citizens of the United States was vast, divisive, and threatening to the social fabric and future of the young country. Faced with meager home dinners and empty lunch boxes, thousands of American children went hungry. By 1900, the majority of states had instituted mandatory schooling up to the age of fourteen, but to keep those kids up to the task of learning, they needed nourishment.

Instigators

ELLEN H. RICHARDS

DR. HARRIET CLISBY

It was known that nutrition was essential to educational success, thanks to the work of **ELLEN H. RICHARDS.** Ellen was a chemist and home economist, the first woman ever granted admission to the Massachusetts Institute of Technology. In the late nineteenth century, she had a hunch that hungry children had a hard time learning, so she conducted a study in nine Boston-area high schools to prove her point. Working in conjunction with the New England Kitchen, an organization focused on poverty and nutrition, she offered students a nutritious noontime meal: options like bread and butter with two cookies, or fish chowder with crackers, available for free or very cheaply. Not quite our memory of cafeteria fare, but her experiment demonstrated that well-fed subjects showed a marked improvement in attention span and knowledge retention. "Many a child has been called stupid," she wrote, "when he was merely hungry."

Before Ellen's research, another Boston woman and one of the country's first female physicians, **DR. HARRIET CLISBY,** noticed the city's women and children suffering from miserable sanitary, working, and living conditions brought on by rapid industrialization and a recent wave of immigration. In 1877, Harriet helped establish the Women's Educational and Industrial Union, which provided support, advocacy, resources, and training in everything from legal aid to professional development. But perhaps one of its most profound contributions to its community and the country came in 1907, when the union used Ellen's research to create what would become a national school lunch program. Union members cooked up hot, nutritional meals in a prep kitchen and shuttled them to local schools.

These badass Bostonian women provided the blueprint from which schools around the country could develop programs of their own. Their passionate advocacy made sure our country could rely on the health of the nation's youth, giving us the well-fed minds and nourished spirits of leaders for generations to come.

Ruth Fertel

1927–2002

*T*HE SIZZLE OF A steak is music to many a diner's ears. But because of one Louisiana woman's life's work, it became the sound of success for thousands of people around the world. At the helm of Ruth's Chris Steak House, Ruth Fertel turned a struggling restaurant into a business empire with a philanthropic spirit.

By the time she was nineteen, Ruth had taken home a degree from Louisiana State University in physics and chemistry with honors. Later, she became a licensed horse trainer—the first woman in Louisiana to do so. When her divorce left her with two children to support on her meager salary as a lab technician at Tulane University, Ruth did something bold. An ad in the New Orleans *Times-Picayune* announced the sale of a failed restaurant, Chris Steak House, in a somewhat seedy neighborhood near the racetrack. Disregarding the advice of those around her, Ruth mortgaged her home and purchased the place in 1965. In a single year, she doubled the restaurant's annual earnings.

Without any experience in the food world, the woman who became known as the Empress of Steak (who stood a petite five foot two) taught herself to butcher massive cuts of meat, mix drinks, and make dressings, and her restaurant began to thrive. But it was a magnet for trouble. Shortly after it opened, Hurricane Betsy devastated the area, and soon after, Ruth took a bullet in the shoulder from a would-be robber. Then, in 1976, a fire destroyed the restaurant. But it took Ruth all of a single week to reopen, rechristening the establishment Ruth's Chris Steak House in an adjacent space, her regulars barely missing a meal.

The world of steak was a man's domain, both at the table and behind the scenes, but that didn't faze Ruth; her restaurant revolutionized the way beef was prepared and served. She was obsessive about quality, following the supply chain to ensure every steak she served was specially dry-aged, and designed a custom broiler that seared her steaks at a whopping 1,800 degrees Fahrenheit. Her signature was topping each steak with a pat of seasoned butter that, when served on a 500-degree slate, sizzled all the way to the table. At a time when fine-dining restaurants were staffed by men, her servers were nearly all female—many of them single mothers, like her. The waitresses were known as the Broads on Broad Street, and they served the area's movers and shakers: politicians, musicians, and artists, as well as the journalists who considered Ruth's ground zero for getting a scoop.

In 1977, Ruth's business began its transformation from a neighborhood hot spot to an international empire, as she turned her exacting standards

into a system that could be reproduced in franchises around the world. Over the two decades that followed, Ruth's Chris grew to encompass more than eighty restaurants from New Orleans to New York, Hong Kong to Dubai. Even as the brand grew, Ruth emphasized the importance of community and equality of opportunity. Her proudest achievement, she said, was watching her franchisees earn their own wealth through her business model.

Today, the Southern Foodways Alliance presents an annual Ruth Fertel Keeper of the Flame Award to honor "a foodways tradition bearer of note," and the philanthropic spirit she instilled in her company persists even now, years after her death, in 2002. In 2009, the original location of the first Ruth's Chris was donated to the university where she once worked and is now the Tulane Community Health Center, providing health care to the neighborhood and those affected by Hurricane Katrina. And the Ruth U. Fertel Foundation focuses on supporting local education from kindergarten to college.

But Ruth wasn't all business. Those closest to her knew a woman ready to crack open a beer and spend time with her restaurant family, and she knew how to throw a party right up until the end. When the mausoleum commissioned to be her final resting place was completed three years before her death, Ruth invited two hundred of her closest friends to celebrate in the cemetery.

Today, Ruth's Chris steaks are still served the way Ruth intended, with a signature sizzle that greets hungry guests all over the globe. And what she built—for her own family, for the Broads on Broad Street, and for franchisees who carry on the company mission—survives in the memory of a bold, ambitious, and visionary woman.

SKILLET-SEARED STRIP STEAK WITH HERB RED WINE BUTTER

SERVES 2 TO 4

EQUIPMENT: Parchment paper, skillet, meat thermometer

HERB RED WINE BUTTER

1 stick unsalted butter, softened

2 tablespoons red wine

½ small shallot, diced

1 teaspoon fresh rosemary, minced

1 teaspoon fresh thyme, minced

SKILLET-SEARED STRIP STEAK

½ teaspoon olive oil

2 lean strip steaks, approximately 12 ounces each

2 teaspoons kosher salt

1 teaspoon cracked black pepper

Make the Herb Red Wine Butter: Place butter in bowl and mash with spoon. Add remaining ingredients and mix with spoon until well combined. Turn butter out onto small sheet of parchment paper. Use parchment to roll and press the butter into a log. Roll butter log up in parchment and refrigerate until solid.

Make the Skillet-Seared Strip Steak: Grease skillet with olive oil and set over high heat. Season both sides of steaks with salt and pepper. Once oil begins to smoke, place steaks on skillet. Sear for 2–3 minutes on each side, until golden brown, then reduce heat. Continue to cook to preferred temperature (check internal temperature with meat thermometer).

Remove steaks from skillet and let stand for 3–5 minutes before serving. Place a slice of Herb Red Wine Butter on each.

MEAT DONENESS GUIDE:

Rare: 120–130°F

Medium Rare: 130–135°F

Medium: 135–145°F

Medium Well: 145–155°F

Well Done: 155°F and up

Leah Chase

1923-PRESENT

LEAH CHASE PROVED that a conversation over gumbo and fried chicken can change the course of America. In the 1960s, the segregated South was deeply divided. But nothing could stop people hungry for a social revolution. Civil rights leaders, the NAACP, the Freedom Riders, and activists, both black and white, needed a place to meet, strategize, and mobilize. That place was Dooky Chase's Restaurant, in New Orleans. And the woman who fed them was Leah.

After graduating from high school with barely a cent to her name, the woman who would come to be known as the Queen of Creole Cooking was expected to follow in the footsteps of the women in her family by working in a factory. But she had no desire to stitch pants pockets all day. After World War II left more jobs than ever before open to women of color, she landed a

gig as a waitress in the disreputable French Quarter. Creoles of color—*gens de couleur*—didn't dare venture near that neck of the woods, even then notorious for debauchery, much less enter it. But Leah paid no mind. Each day she passed the houses of ill repute on her way to work at a whites-only restaurant. The job filled her with wonder: she'd never before seen people sit down for a meal and be waited on.

In 1946, Leah married musician Edgar "Dooky" Chase, Jr., whose family owned Dooky Chase's Restaurant. Despite her lack of formal training, she took over in the kitchen, mastering traditional Creole and Southern foods like gumbo, red beans and rice, fried chicken, and peach cobbler. But she also taught herself to cook the dishes she'd served diners at whites-only restaurants—decadent French classics, like Shrimp Clemenceau, with fine wines to go with them.

Leah turned Dooky Chase's into the city's first fine-dining restaurant welcoming to African Americans, complete with white tablecloths, sparkling glasses, and gleaming silverware. For Leah, hospitality was not simply emulating the things she'd seen in whites-only establishments; it was about showing respect for New Orleans's black population.

Located in historic Tremé—the oldest African-American neighborhood in the United States—Dooky Chase's quickly became a safe haven for the black community and a club for those who sought to end segregation. An upstairs room sheltered secret meetings where Martin Luther King, Jr., and the Freedom Riders planned the Montgomery bus boycott over Leah's bowls of gumbo. To keep the police at bay, Leah's mother-in-law made sure to slip plenty of extra plates and sandwiches their way. Over the years, Dooky Chase's hosted numerous icons of the civil rights movement—the Reverend A. L. Davis, Thurgood Marshall, and King sat at its integrated tables. Amid the changing world around them, they knew they could rely on one thing: Leah's food and hospitality to get them through it.

Because African Americans weren't allowed at many of the city's restaurants, they mostly entertained at home. Dooky Chase's changed all that. It became the place to commemorate anniversaries and graduations, to take your girl on a first date, to routinely enjoy delicious lunches. It was the only place of its kind—a black-owned, fine-dining restaurant—and a lively one at that, where folks went to see and be seen. It was known simply as "the restaurant" to regulars and gained a following among musicians, athletes, political figures, and black artists; Leah's was at one time considered the best collection of African-American art in New Orleans. She befriended many of her prestigious guests, later even hosting Presidents George W. Bush and Barack Obama.

For seventy-plus years, Leah's commitment to serving her community has remained steadfast, and both she and the restaurant are legendary. Recognized with honorary degrees and accolades, including the 2016 James Beard Foundation Lifetime Achievement Award, Leah's contribution to the black community and the city of New Orleans made her an icon and inspired Disney's first African-American princess, Tiana, in the film *The Princess and the Frog.* Ray Charles sang about going to Dooky Chase's in his song "Early in the Morning."

Leah is often photographed wearing a brilliant smile. Her guests revel in her warmth and hospitality. But beneath her Southern charm and cloud of white hair are the sharp wit and tongue of a daring woman who wouldn't let a little something like public opinion change her mind about what was right.

Women of Whiskey

MULTIPLE ERAS

THE HISTORY OF WHISKEY is far more complex than a perfectly balanced Manhattan. In eras past, making spirits was a way to sterilize water as well as preserve grain crops. Whiskey has been used as a remedy for everything from toothaches to pneumonia (not to mention quite a lot of heartbreak). And while somewhere along the way the drink became associated with traditional masculinity, it has long been women ensuring that the stuff got made. There's even evidence that it was a woman who invented the first still. Today, a growing number of world-renowned distilleries are female-owned and -operated. But it all started with a few who blazed the trail.

Instigators

RITA
TAKETSURU

HELEN
CUMMING

BESSIE
WILLIAMSON

MARY DOWLING

CATHERINE
SPEARS FRYE
CARPENTER

CATHERINE SPEARS FRYE CARPENTER Catherine not only operated a commercial distillery in Kentucky but also put down on paper the first recipe for sour mash whiskey, in 1818. Legend has it the original directions were scribbled on the back of a family Bible—appropriate, as it became gospel for whiskey-making generations ever since.

MARY DOWLING Mary assumed control of Waterfill and Frazier Distillery after her husband died. When Prohibition threatened the family business, she simply packed up and moved her Kentucky distillery to Mexico. From there, she slaked Americans' thirst for whiskey during the dry years. Some believe that the onetime limitation of the name "bourbon" to the liquor made in Bourbon County, Kentucky, was established to thwart Mary as she remained in Mexico and competed with American whiskey makers.

BESSIE WILLIAMSON What began as a summer job in 1934 became a lifelong career and a worldwide legacy when Bessie Williamson took a job as a typist at Laphroaig, the famed Scotch whiskey producer. Over the course of twenty years, she worked closely with the distillery's owner, Ian Hunter, moving from the typewriter keys to the helm, eventually managing the entire operation and guiding it through World War II, when the distillery was used to store weapons. When Ian died, in 1954, he left the business in her capable hands. She brought Laphroaig into international markets, especially the United States, and helped to establish the identity of single malt Scotch as a category.

RITA TAKETSURU In 1920, Masataka Taketsuru arrived in Scotland in search of the secrets of Scotch distillers, but he left with the love of his life. Jessie Roberta—Rita, as she was known—moved to Japan with Masataka while he worked to build the Japanese whiskey industry. He eventually established his own business, Nikka Whisky Distilling. Despite some resistance to Rita and Masataka's bicultural union, Rita Taketsuru earned the respect of the Japanese people—not to mention the title Mother of Japanese Whiskey—by financially supporting her husband as he applied what he'd learned in her homeland. A street in Yoichi where the distillery is based bears her name, and the couple's story has even been immortalized as a television drama. But the real legacy lives in every bottle.

HELEN CUMMING In the early 1800s, Helen Cumming married a former whiskey smuggler named John. Perhaps his rebellious nature was part of the attraction; Helen herself would become legendary for her lawbreaking. After John founded a more legitimate business, Cardhu Distillery, Helen worked to evade the hefty Scottish taxes on distilling. While John toiled in the fields of their farm, Helen headed up production and sales. When tax collectors came to call, she hid any evidence of a distillery, covering up the odors of whiskey fermentation with the aroma of freshly baked bread. She distracted them with tea and other treats, and sent up a flag to alert fellow small producers in her area. Helen remained involved until she was well into her nineties, though she passed off the operations to another woman in the family: her daughter-in-law, Elizabeth. Today, their whiskey is blended into Johnnie Walker, and the business is aboveboard—and Helen's legacy fills many a Scotch lover's glass.

Women in Media

TWENTIETH CENTURY - PRESENT

JUDITH JONES Identifying talent in others is an invaluable skill. Judith Jones made a career as a lifelong advocate for female culinary voices, empowering women whose passion and talents might have otherwise been overlooked and forever redefining how Americans cooked. An editor at the famed New York publishing house Alfred A. Knopf, she was a fierce advocate for, and careful editor of, her many celebrated writers, distilling the essence of their culinary mastery into relatable language for American audiences. Through her stable of authors, Judith built a diverse canon of food writing that transcended what was considered approachable cooking: Julia Child, Madhur Jaffrey, Edna Lewis, Claudia Roden, Irene Kuo, and Lidia Bastianich were just a few of the influential voices encouraged by her expert, insightful editing.

MASTERING THE ART OF FRENCH COOKING

THE TASTE OF COUNTRY COOKING

An Invitation to INDIAN COOKING

THE KEY TO CHINESE COOKING

The New Book of Middle Eastern Food

LIDIA'S MASTERING THE ART OF ITALIAN CUISINE

JUDITH JONES

ELIZABETH DAVID

RUTH REICHL

CLAUDIA WU

CHERRYBOMBE

KERRY DIAMOND

It wasn't only keen intuition that set Judith apart, but her curiosity. She anticipated far in advance the kinds of cuisines that would come to be international favorites, and saw each book as a chance to build trust between her authors and readers. She elevated the status of cookbooks in America, and also that of the typically female professions of cookbook writers and editors, once considered the lowest rung on publishing's ladder.

ELIZABETH DAVID Whirlwind travel, torrid affairs, and delectable eats: Elizabeth David was a rebel well before her time. The Englishwoman who saved Britain from stodgy food lived a life that could rival any screenplay. Seduced by the flavors of France while studying art at the Sorbonne in the 1930s, Elizabeth returned home to find life in England bland by comparison. Years spent in Greece, France, Sicily, and Egypt had her longing for European flavors. Elizabeth poured ideas for those dishes into 1950's *Book of Mediterranean Food* and painted an intimate portrait of the cultures that captivated her. Her books, including subsequent takes on France and Italy, offered a cosmopolitan escape to a British society burdened with the aftermath of war. Her heavenly recipes and cheeky descriptions delighted and invigorated the public, earning her the moniker Most Revered Goddess of Cooking from the British press. Her work would later make it around the world, inspiring culinary wanderlust in cultures far beyond her own.

RUTH REICHL Ruth Reichl knows good food. And as a restaurant critic for the *Los Angeles Times* and then the *New York Times*, followed by ten years as editor in chief of *Gourmet* magazine, the novelist and cookbook author has spent decades telling us exactly what it is and where to find it. Ruth demystified the world of fine dining, exposing the truths of the restaurant industry and forcing even the most high-end establishments to examine their own snobbery—and often their insidious sexism. At *Gourmet*, she steered the once-recipe-focused magazine toward journalistic features that made readers aware of the cultural importance of the food they ate. Through her diverse culinary career, she transitioned from chef and restaurant owner to memoirist to food novelist, never forsaking her honest view of the relationship between those who cook and those who eat.

KERRY DIAMOND AND CLAUDIA WU (*CHERRY BOMBE* MAGAZINE) If it's broke, fix it. That's exactly what *Cherry Bombe* founders, Kerry Diamond and Claudia Wu, did. Frustrated by the lack of female coverage in food media, the two women, both with a background in fashion publications, launched their biannual indie magazine in 2013. With fierce cover girls like Padma Lakshmi, Kristen Kish, Chrissy Teigen, and Nigella Lawson, *Cherry Bombe* turned a brilliant spotlight on women making culinary waves. The stylish magazine, with its characteristic high-contrast photography and tongue-in-cheek vibe, champions the sensibility and diversity of female food connoisseurs. Building on bold, feminine energy, the brand transcends print, providing its dedicated readership—known as the Bombe Squad—with a podcast, merchandise, and an annual conference for women in the food industry, the Cherry Bombe Jubilee. Kerry and Claudia's success has proven that feminist media can enact change, demonstrating to those who pushed women to the margins of their magazines that there is real hunger for women in food.

Nitza Villapol

1923–1998

WASTE NOT, WANT NOT," the old saying goes. But Nitza Villapol proved to the people of Cuba that you don't need a lot to live abundantly. Throughout her career, her countrymen and -women faced political hardship and dire economic circumstances beyond their control, but Nitza's recipes and teachings showed them they could still lead healthy, joyful lives.

Born in 1923 to Cuban immigrants to the United States, Nitza learned to cook from her mother, who emphasized efficiency in the kitchen. Her methods preserved resources and encouraged Nitza to spend less time in the kitchen, and more time out in the world. And boy, did she get out there. The family later relocated to Cuba, and in the late 1940s—a decade and a half before Julia Child entered a single living room—Nitza made her small-screen debut on Cuban television in *Cocina al Minuto* as one of the first food personalities in television history. She went on to pen two books by the same name.

Cocina al Minuto was published in separate volumes—the first in 1954, and the follow-up in 1991. A comparison of the two gives readers an idea of how Cuban life changed over the course of those decades. In 1959, Fidel Castro came to power, and by the early 1960s, trade to Cuba had dramatically dwindled under the U.S. embargo. The 1991 edition, full of creative improvisations developed to cope with extremely limited resources, reflects these scarcities. Nitza, who had trained as a nutritionist, passed on tips for how to make use of food waste and to eat a balanced diet with cheap, plant-based meals.

Nitza was one of the few broadcast personalities to maintain her television show throughout the Castro regime. It remained a beacon for a frightened and confused population, who looked to her to let them know that life would go on. All you've got for dinner is plantain peels? No problem. Her show demonstrated how to season and cook them, noting how nutritious and satisfying they could still be. But Nitza wasn't the prim and proper ideal of a domestic goddess we might imagine today. She was a revolutionary, not shy about her disdain for the American influence on Cuban cooking and culture. It's believed that Nitza, like her father, was a communist, and her cooking was a study in thriving under communism. While many see her work as an inspiration, Nitza also came under fire for her views; there was even speculation that her show and books were propaganda for Castro's regime.

Regardless of her politics, Nitza's influence on the culinary heritage of Cuba endures. For a country facing food insecurity, her creativity wasn't just a way to freshen up old dishes. It helped empower the Cuban people. It showed them that limitation did not mean deprivation. Many Cubans who escaped the island under Castro carried her cookbooks with them. The texts still provided a connection to home, practical instructions for maintaining traditions when so much had to be left behind. Within Cuban culture, both on the island and abroad, Nitza's work continues to connect culture and family, and proves that creativity, for the sake of health, of culture, of family, will never go to waste.

COCONUT-CRUSTED PLANTAINS WITH LIME GARLIC MINT SAUCE

SERVES 4

EQUIPMENT: Small chopper or food processor, medium frying pan

LIME GARLIC MINT SAUCE

¼ cup extra-virgin olive oil

3 cloves garlic

Juice of ½ lime

1 tablespoon honey

1 tablespoon mint, chopped (approximately 8 leaves)

COCONUT-CRUSTED PLANTAINS

1 cup all-purpose flour

2 eggs, whisked

1 cup unsweetened coconut flakes

2 large ripe plantains

Canola oil

Sea salt

Cracked black pepper

Make the Lime Garlic Mint Sauce: In small chopper or food processor, mix all ingredients together. Set aside.

Make the Coconut-Crusted Plantains: Put flour, whisked eggs, and coconut flakes into three separate bowls. Cut ends off plantains and remove peel by slicing it lengthwise and slipping it off. Cut angled, ¼-inch-thick slices of plantain—roughly twelve per plantain. Pour 3 tablespoons canola oil into medium frying pan on medium heat. Dredge slices of plantain in flour (shake off excess), then dip in eggs and coat thoroughly with coconut flakes. Fry crusted plantain slices until coconut is a rich brown, making sure to flip and cook both sides. Remove burnt bits of coconut from pan and replenish oil as needed. Transfer fried plantain slices to plate or tray lined with paper towels to absorb excess oil.

Place about six coconut-crusted plantain slices on each of four small plates. Drizzle Lime Garlic Mint Sauce over and around plantains. Finish with sprinkle of sea salt and cracked black pepper.

Sarah Josepha Hale

1788–1879

TODAY, **THANKSGIVING** is practically synonymous with feasting, but before Sarah Josepha Hale, it was just another Thursday in November. Though the arrival of settlers to the Americas was marked with small celebrations observed in varying parts of the country, there was no consistent Thanksgiving tradition.

But Sarah knew the power of communication. She was one of the country's first female novelists, a poet, and the editor of a women's magazine. Though better known as the mother of Thanksgiving, she also authored the classic nursery rhyme "Mary Had a Little Lamb." Sarah spent much of her long career (lasting until she was eighty-nine) working for women's advancement and education. She was vocal in her support of Vassar College, one of the first women's colleges in the country.

She argued fiercely for a shared national day of thanks, both as a celebration of family and of unity across state lines. Her first novel, *Northwood*, dedicated the better part of a chapter to the joys of Thanksgiving as an annual custom. She wrote editorials in her magazine urging its adoption as a national holiday, and autumnal issues included recipes for Turkey Day staples, as well as stories, poems, and cooking advice for the holiday. But she didn't stop there. As the celebration gained popularity throughout the country, Sarah petitioned governors, legislators, and even the president and secretary of state. And after the outbreak of the Civil War, the need for a national day on which to suspend hostilities and express gratitude became obvious. In 1863, President Lincoln issued an official proclamation, and the holiday was born. Each November, we express gratitude for a great many things, but it is Sarah Josepha Hale—her tireless, ambitious campaign born from a desire for tradition and national unity—whom we can thank for Thanksgiving itself.

Women of Tea

SEVENTEENTH CENTURY-PRESENT

CATHERINE OF BRAGANZA England and tea are so connected that most would presume the island nation is responsible for its popularity. But it was a Portuguese princess, Catarina Henriqueta de Bragança—more commonly known as Catherine of Braganza—who inspired Britain's love for a good cuppa.

In 1662, the British crown was heavily in debt, and Charles II needed a wife and money. He chose Catherine, the eldest daughter of the king of Portugal. Her dowry was extensive; her hand came along with stores of exotic spices, loose-leaf tea, and other luxuries, as well as control over the port city of Bombay, a stronghold for British trade through the East India Company.

Tea already existed in England before the queen consort's arrival but was taxed heavily, making it extremely expensive and available only to the wealthiest. Because of access to Chinese ports where tea was traded, Portugal's elite were already accustomed to drinking tea, using beautiful (and

AVANTIKA JALAN

LASSI TAMANG

CATHERINE OF BRAGANZA

TEA

BRITISH EAST IND
TRADING COMP

FINE TEA LE

pricey) porcelain cups and saucers, teapots, and dishes for sugar. Catherine brought this fashionable style of tea service to her new country, enchanting the court. The aristocracy's new obsession trickled down to England's upper class. Smugglers sidestepped steep taxation, and tea drinking among commoners gained popularity in the eighteenth century. Today, Britain's love of tea is nothing short of a national obsession. Eighty-four percent of the population enjoys a spot of tea daily—that's over sixty billion cups each year.

INDIA'S BUDDING TEA WOMEN: AVANTIKA JALAN AND LASSI TAMANG

Tea cultivation may conjure bucolic images of lush landscapes and women plucking two leaves and a bud. But the reality is far less idyllic. Female workers—who make up over 50 percent of the labor force in the production of tea, the second-largest industry in India—are subject to subpar conditions, performing backbreaking labor while filling few managerial positions.

However, the number of women assuming roles as small tea producers and factory managers today in India is growing, and many have been empowered to attain financial independence. Founder and managerial director Avantika Jalan started the socially responsible organic tea line Mana Organics on Chota Tingrai, her family's tea estate. A fourth-generation tea producer, she's hiring women not just for physical labor, but for roles in field management and administrative duties.

Lassi Tamang shattered the industry's glass ceiling when she became one of the first female tea factory managers in Darjeeling. Her family didn't have a connection to tea, like most men in cushy managerial roles or women who inherit underpaid tea-harvesting jobs from their mothers. After completing a postcollegiate tea management course, she applied for a factory assistant position at the crème de la crème of Darjeeling tea estates, Jungpana, whose tea has been served to royalty. Remarkably, she was accepted, and after seven years, Lassi's dedication and hard work paid off: she was promoted to factory manager, the first woman to hold this position at Jungpana.

The women ascending the ladder of India's tea business prove that they can be more than bonded laborers. Avantika is creating a level playing field, enabling women to achieve positions of responsibility and capitalize on far-reaching opportunities. Lassi is taking education into her own hands, demonstrating that a woman can be an authority. Both are leading a new generation that's giving the tea world a true taste of what it's made of.

TEA, MEET SUGAR

If diamonds or Italian truffles have taught us anything, it's that the more rare and expensive an item, the more we want it. No two commodities screamed luxury and wealth in seventeenth- and eighteenth-century Europe like sugar and tea. But the popularity of sweet tea fueled one of the darkest movements in human existence: the Atlantic slave trade. To meet insatiable demand for the "white gold" sweetening high society's cups of afternoon tea, millions of Africans were shipped to the Caribbean and parts of South America to toil on sugarcane plantations. At the turn of the eighteenth century, British abolitionists sparked a boycott of sugar produced by enslaved labor in the West Indies. In response, sales of slave-grown sugar plunged in Britain—the leading slave-trading nation—as sales from India spiked. Though it would take several decades to end slave trading after Britain's 1807 prohibition of the practice, the efforts of abolitionists and antislavery associations led by women fueled public outcry and hastened the end of these crimes against humanity.

Women of Prohibition

1920s

WOMEN ARE OFTEN REMEMBERED as the instigators of the Eighteenth Amendment, which prohibited the sale of alcohol in the United States from 1920 to 1933, but they were just as active in skirting it. Whether taking advantage of laws forbidding police from searching them to secretly stashing a flask to building massive empires of speakeasies and smuggling houses, the female sex undeniably played a role in keeping Americans drinking.

GERTRUDE "CLEO" LYTHGOE Before Prohibition, the Bahama Queen—Gertrude "Cleo" Lythgoe—was employed by a British liquor importer. After the ratification of the Eighteenth Amendment, her boss sent her to the Bahamas, where she took the opportunity to set up her own shop and

"SPANISH MARIE" WAITE

"MOONSHINE MARY" WAZENIAK

PAULINE MORTON SABIN

GLORIA DE CESARES

GERTRUDE "CLEO" LYTHGOE

became one of the most infamous liquor suppliers of the era. Cleo is remembered as a brash, pistol-toting boss lady who'd threaten anyone who insulted her liquor with instant death. Her business acumen, success in the trade, and general reputation as a wild woman helped her command international attention.

"MOONSHINE MARY" WAZENIAK   At age thirty-four, Illinois-born Mary Wazeniak became the first woman to be arrested for selling lethal liquor when one of the patrons at her illegal speakeasy walked out and fell down dead. She was convicted of manslaughter, earning the nickname Moonshine Mary in the press and spending a year in prison. Her brush with the law brought new attention to the dangers of unregulated alcohol, which became a major part of the argument for Prohibition's repeal.

"SPANISH MARIE" WAITE   When her husband, Charlie, King of the Rum Runners, died in 1926, Marie Waite took over his robust smuggling business. Reportedly a ruthless businesswoman with a fiery personality, known as Spanish Marie thanks to her Latin roots, she wielded daggers and pistols with swagger and smuggled rum from Cuba to the United States via a small fleet of ships. Marie was successful not only at dodging the authorities, but at operating one of the most lucrative rackets of the day. She raked in nearly $1 million over her career, a feat all the more astonishing given that it lasted only about two years before she vanished from the scene.

GLORIA DE CESARES With the founding of her business, the Gloria Steamship Company, the ambitious young Gloria de Cesares began working to smuggle booze into the United States. Unfortunately for her aspirations, one of her ships sailing to America was intercepted, and authorities discovered more than ten thousand cases of Scotch, worth more than a million in today's dollars. But officials were feeling generous—and a little out of their depth, given the international waters in which they discovered her—and Gloria got off with a stern warning. It was advice she apparently took to heart; she retired from the game soon after.

PAULINE MORTON SABIN While many women were profiting from illegal bootlegging businesses, one was much more concerned about the law—specifically, changing it. Pauline Morton Sabin founded the Women's Organization for National Prohibition Reform. She felt that Prohibition had failed to curb the nation's appetite for drinking as well as creating a cultural disrespect for law and order. She rejected the idea that all women were in support of the temperance movement, and she was right; her organization grew to 1.5 million members in less than two years. Though Pauline was a New York socialite, she recruited immigrants and members of blue-collar families to represent a true cross section of American women. Those of us who like to tipple can raise a toast to Pauline: without her work to have Prohibition repealed, we might not be able to fill our glasses today.

Girl Scouts of America

TWENTIETH CENTURY—PRESENT

IN 1917, THE GIRL SCOUTS of Muskogee, Oklahoma, were in need of funds. In the spirit of social outreach, a core Scout value, they wanted to make gifts for World War I soldiers. But they needed cash to pay for them, so they asked themselves, as the suffragettes had nearly half a century before them (page 89), what better way to get it than a bake sale? What they didn't know was their little cookie enterprise would ignite more than a few oven pilot lights—it would become a food phenomenon.

It was only five years after Juliette Gordon Low founded the Girl Scouts with a group of eighteen girls in Savannah, Georgia, that the first cookie was sold. Her objective was to create an environment that provided young girls with inspiration, education, a sense of adventure, and a supportive community. She hoped to prepare them with "courage, confidence, and character," as well as leadership skills that would transcend their time with

the group and follow them into adulthood. And cookies, it turned out, were to become a major part of growing up as a Girl Scout.

In 1922, the Girl Scouts' magazine, *The American Girl,* published a recipe for a simple sugar cookie and suggested troops sell it to raise money. But cookie sales proved so popular that the girls couldn't keep up with demand: by 1936, the Girl Scouts had to license their recipe to commercial bakers.

What began as a simple fund-raising program became a cultural cornerstone. Today, more than 200 *million* boxes of Girl Scout cookies are sold every season. But you can also purchase an insane array of Girl Scout cookie–inspired products: ice cream, yogurt, breakfast cereal, chewing gum, granola bars, coffee creamer, herbal tea—even lip gloss. And the cookies themselves have evolved according to trends, adding variations like the S'mores variety in 2017 to the classic lineup: crispy, addictive Thin Mints; chewy, toasty Samoas; crunchy, peanut-buttery Tagalongs—and so many more. Seriously... who's got a box?

Fueled by cookies, the Girl Scouts have been a source of female empowerment for more than a century, seeing generations of women through multiple waves of feminism, from the fight for suffrage, to the women's liberation movement of the 1960s, to watching one of its alumnae become the first female candidate for president of the United States. According to the Girl Scout website, more than half of Girl Scouts who went on to careers in business remember cookie selling as foundational to their success.

The Scouts' cookie cash has been used to support communities globally. Today the cookies, which find their way into more than 50 million households in the United States alone, are tied to the organization's G.I.R.L. Agenda: transforming its participants into "Go-getters, Innovators, Risk-takers, and Leaders." Juliette's original vision may not have included baked goods, but because she gave her Girl Scouts the space to create and strategize, they had the tools to secure their own legacy all around the world. The ability to spin a little sugar into magic—to the tune of $800 million a year—is some serious G.I.R.L. power.

GIRL SCOUT ICEBOX CAKE

SERVES 8 TO 10

EQUIPMENT: 9-inch springform cake pan

3 boxes Girl Scout cookies

2 cups heavy whipping cream, chilled

½ cup confectioners' sugar

½ teaspoon pure vanilla extract

Coarsely chop cookies. Transfer to bowl.

Combine cold heavy whipping cream, confectioners' sugar, and vanilla extract in metal bowl of stand mixer with whip attachment (you can also use hand mixer or whip by hand). Start on low to mix all ingredients, then increase speed to medium. Whip cream just until smooth, stiff peaks form (cream will appear grainy if overwhipped). Remove bowl from mixer. Reserve 1 cup whipped cream in separate bowl, cover, and refrigerate.

On bottom of springform pan, spread layer of cookies, using fingers to press them together to create even base. Spread ¼- to ½-inch layer of remaining whipped cream on top. Add another layer of cookies, followed by whipped cream, then cookies (three layers of cookies and two layers of whipped cream). Cover top of icebox cake with plastic wrap, making sure it touches entire surface, and freeze.

When ready to serve, lightly rewhip reserved whipped cream. Remove plastic wrap from icebox cake and spread whipped cream over entire surface. Place in freezer for 30 minutes to set top layer of whipped cream. Slide knife around perimeter of cake to release edges from springform before opening clamp. Gently lift pan base out from springform mold.

Garnish icebox cake with your choice of toppings. Before slicing, be sure to warm knife in hot water. After each slice, clean knife and rewarm for neat slices of cake.

NOTE *This is one of the simplest preparations for a fast and fun dessert. Any cookie will work in a pinch, and we've provided some ideas for flavor inspiration below. A standard Trefoil shortbread is a perfect starting point.*

MAKE IT YOUR OWN WITH SOME FLAVOR INSPIRATION

Thin Mints: Spoon dollops of strawberry jam on cookie layers. Garnish with fresh strawberry slices before serving.

Samoas: Drizzle caramel sauce over cookie layers. Garnish with crushed smoked almonds and dust with instant espresso powder.

Tagalongs: Drizzle top with balsamic reduction and garnish with salted, toasted bread crumbs.

Inven

tors

THESE WOMEN CREATED
GAME-CHANGING MACHINES,
PROCESSES, AND RECIPES WE
COULDN'T LIVE WITHOUT.

Madame Barbe-Nicole Clicquot

1777-1866

The world is in perpetual motion, and we must invent the things of tomorrow. One must go before others, be determined and exacting, and let your intelligence direct your life. Act with audacity.

—MADAME BARBE-NICOLE CLICQUOT, GRANDE DAME OF CHAMPAGNE

MADAME BARBE-NICOLE CLICQUOT is the woman responsible for Champagne as we know it. Without her groundbreaking innovation, refusal to accept limitations imposed on women, and shrewd business savvy, celebrations for the last three centuries would have lacked that certain fizz. Her mission, beyond making the finest Champagne possible, was to make it available around the world.

The daughter of a baron and textile industry tycoon, Barbe had access to a superior education. And in 1798, when she married François Clicquot, she discovered how she would put her mind to use. François was the heir to Maison Clicquot—then a small winemaking operation in Reims, France. Barbe and François saw an opportunity to expand the business into sparkling wines, but he died suddenly, leaving her a twenty-seven-year-old single mother. After François's death, Barbe's father-in-law wanted to shut down his wine operation; what would become known as the Napoleonic Wars were under way, and business was dismal.

But Barbe was passionate about continuing what she and François began. She persuaded her father-in-law not only to allow her to take over the business, but to invest in it as well. Now the first woman at the head of a major vineyard, Barbe apprenticed herself to a master winemaker and worked diligently to understand the craft.

Barbe didn't invent Champagne; other vineyards created sparkling wine, but they were relatively unpopular. Those wines were bottled with lees—or residual yeast—which made them cloudy and unstable. And because of the climate in the Champagne region, colder weather could interfere with their fermentation in the bottle. So Barbe came up with a foolproof method: the riddling process, in which the bottles were placed upside down, allowing the yeasts to collect and be removed. The result was a crystal-clear bottle with a stable and consistent taste. Veuve Clicquot would become the gold standard for Champagne everywhere.

As the Napoleonic Wars came to an end, and Russians found a reason to celebrate, they bought up stores of fine French wine. Barbe smuggled a supply of her Veuve Clicquot first to Amsterdam, then to Russia, and edged out other winemakers looking to sell to the Russian market. Her sweet wine appealed to the Russian palate, and after Tsar Alexander tasted it and declared that Veuve Clicquot was the only Champagne for him, demand exploded.

When fraudsters came forward, attempting to take advantage of Champagne's massive popularity with high society, Barbe took them to court but resolved to set her wines apart from the competition with more than just flavor. Rather than bottling Veuve Clicquot in unmarked bottles, as was the norm for winemakers, she designed the iconic yellow label we still recognize today.

Madame Clicquot was a brilliant business mind, an innovator, a marketer, and a genius of branding long before we had entire agencies dedicated to such things. She demanded quality and knew how to communicate it; her label is an enduring symbol of luxury and excellence—and of her own temerity.

Women of Beer

• MULTIPLE ERAS •

HISTORICALLY SPEAKING, beer has been a woman's work—and a woman's drink—all over the world. Whether to make water safe to drink, to serve as a dietary supplement, or even for use in religious ceremonies, women have been creating beer long before Homer Simpson ever laid his yellow hands on a single can of Duff.

CHINA Evidence dating back to between 7000 and 5600 BCE suggests that the legendary Yi Di, the wife of the Xia dynasty's King Yu, created the culture's first alcohol, an early beer brewed with rice, honey, and fruit, around 2100 BCE.

ANCIENT MESOPOTAMIA Complete with a recipe, a Sumerian hymn dated circa 1800 BCE celebrates the goddess of beer, Ninkasi. In Mesopotamia, brewing was a woman's work, thought to earn her special protection from the gods. Some historians believe ancient Babylonian brewers may have been the world's first business owners, since they kept their books with the earliest known system of writing.

EGYPT Ancient Egyptians worshipped their own goddess of brewing, Tenenit, by enjoying a honeyed beer brewed by women. But throwing back a beer wasn't purely recreation; it was sustenance. In fact, the workers who built the famous Pyramids were often paid in pints. Later, Cleopatra experienced extreme unpopularity when she imposed a tax on beer, allegedly to curb public drunkenness.

ANCIENT GREECE AND ROME Wine was a stronger beverage, and so considered a man's drink, while beer was seen as suitable for the lower classes—and for women. Roman women were even encouraged by Pliny the Elder to use its foam "for cosmetic purposes," as a skin conditioner.

GERMANY Perhaps most important to the history of brewing was Saint Hildegard von Bingen, a German nun and herbalist who, in the twelfth century, discovered that hops could act as a natural preservative. The use of hops not only forever altered beer's flavor but produced the global beer industry, as the beverage's lengthened shelf life allowed it to be commercially brewed and distributed.

ENGLAND Before the thirteenth century AD, female brewers—or "brewsters"—were the primary producers of beer in home kitchens; beer was considered food and an integral part of a meal. When there were leftovers,

a broomstick wrapped with hop wreaths at the door let passersby know beer was for sale inside. But women who ran alehouses were often accused of bewitching their patrons to imbibe heavily and act in undignified ways. So much for personal responsibility, dudes.

FINLAND Recipes for *sahti*, a centuries-old beer made with juniper, hops, and rye, have been passed from mother to daughter through the ages. Legend has it that Finnish women invented beer by mixing the saliva of a wild bear with honey.

SCANDINAVIA It is believed that Viking conquests were fueled largely by vast quantities of beer brewed by women. Imbibe and conquer.

IRELAND Though women were outlawed from ordering beer without a male chaperone in twentieth-century Ireland, Saint Brigid of Kildare in the sixth century was reputed to be able to turn water into beer. Now *that's* a cool party trick.

SOUTH AMERICA *Chicha*, a beerlike beverage made from maize, cassava, quinoa, peanuts, or tubers, is still made today. But centuries ago, women chewed the ingredients, allowing the enzymes in their saliva to break down the starches, then fermented their spit in clay pots.

EARLY AMERICA During America's colonial era, women were the brewers in their new communities, making beer in home kitchens from indigenous ingredients like corn, wheat, pumpkin, oats, and honey.

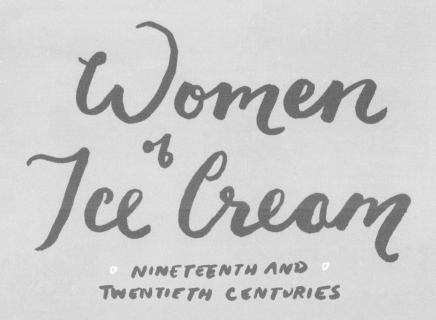

Women of Ice Cream

Nineteenth and Twentieth Centuries

NANCY JOHNSON AND AGNES MARSHALL   Though the driver of the neighborhood-trawling ice cream truck might always be referred to as the "ice cream man," there's no doubt he'd be piloting his rig along the unemployment line had it not been for the ingenuity of women.

Ice cream can be traced as far back as ancient Greece, where snow and ice were flavored with fruit and honey, and it's gone on to be a favorite of kings and emperors across cultures and eras. In America, its history of fans includes everyone from Founding Fathers like Ben Franklin to presidents (Washington is said to have dropped two hundred dollars—that's more than five thousand dollars in today's cash—on the stuff) and first ladies, Mary Todd Lincoln and Dolley Madison among them. Mrs. Madison is said to have been turned on to the frozen treat when a server tipped her off to a freed slave named Aunt Sallie Shadd, who ran a catering company. Dolley loved Aunt Sallie's ice cream desserts so much that she served them at her White House dinners.

NANCY JOHNSON

AB MARSHALL
ICES PLAIN AND FANCY
FANCY ICES

GROCERY LIST
☑ 1 PINT CREAM
☑ 1 LB SUGAR
☐ 8 EGGS
☐ ARROWROOT

AGNES MARSHALL

For most of history, ice cream was a delicacy available only to the wealthy. Ingredients were pricey, and before the invention of freezers, creating it involved painstakingly collecting ice and snow. It wasn't until the late nineteenth and early twentieth centuries that ice cream found a broader audience, when Nancy Johnson, a Philadelphia housewife, revolutionized the way it was made. Instead of stirring cream and sugar in a bowl placed in a bucket of ice, she thought to add rock salt to the ice to aid in quick freezing and developed a hand-cranked machine to churn the cream. The result was a far creamier finished product, frozen in a fraction of the time and with far less labor and expensive ice. Her patent was issued in 1846, and to this day modern ice cream machines still work in pretty much the same way.

On the other side of the Atlantic, less than ten years after Nancy's patent was issued, Agnes Marshall would revolutionize the ice cream recipe itself. By the time Agnes died, in 1905, she'd earned the nickname Queen of Ices.

Agnes's published books included *Ices Plain and Fancy* and *Fancy Ices*, with instructions for more familiar flavors like vanilla and pistachio, as well as some that even avant-garde ice cream makers might find eyebrow-raising— like cucumber and brown bread. Recipes also kept readers' economic reach in mind, because in Agnes's eyes, everyone deserved to enjoy ice cream. A single recipe might have options for four different bases, ranging from "very rich"—made with a pint of cream, a pound of sugar, and eight egg yolks—to "cheap," which called for the more affordable pint of milk, quarter pound of sugar, and half an ounce of arrowroot as a stabilizer. Agnes's books were so popular that London even saw a spike in ice importing from Norway.

Beyond instructions for ice cream itself, there's evidence that Agnes's was the first recipe for the ice cream cone. Directions for making Cornets with Cream were published in her *Mrs. A. B. Marshall's Book of Cookery* in 1888, six years before the cone's often-cited U.S. debut in 1904. And Nancy wasn't the only lady tinkering with ice cream tools. In 1885 Agnes received her own patent for an ice cream machine, which could reportedly whip up a pint in five minutes flat.

Women of Coffee

NINETEENTH AND TWENTIETH CENTURIES AND TODAY

MELITTA BENTZ If you're one of the many millions of people around the world who've ever taken pleasure in a perfectly made cup of joe, there's an enterprising German woman for you to thank: Melitta Bentz, inventor of the paper coffee filter.

Over the course of the twentieth century, coffee, once a delicacy available only to the affluent, became a defining part of everyone's morning ritual. But earlier coffee bore little resemblance to what we drink today. Methods of making it were inconsistent and inefficient. Cloth filters existed, but they were expensive and failed to fully separate the grounds, producing a bitter cup muddied by unpleasant sediment and a real pain to clean up.

MELITTA
BENTZ

AIDA
BATLLE

ERNA
KNUTSEN

Melitta had had it with the process, so she took a page from her son's book—literally. Perforating a sheet of his notebook blotting paper and setting it inside a metal cup, she put the grounds inside the paper and poured hot water over it, a disposable, easy-to-clean system that produced far superior coffee. Melitta's product was not only the basis for the drip coffeemakers of today, but the early prototype for the pour-over process so popular in specialty coffee shops.

With just 72 Reichsmark cents, the equivalent of just 30 dollars today as start-up money, Melitta set up shop in her apartment in Dresden, Germany. Her design won awards for its ingenuity, and by 1928, just twenty years after its founding, her business had grown from her husband and sons to a staff of more than eighty people. Beyond the cup, Melitta made great strides in changing standards for workers. Her business was one of the first to offer more than two weeks of vacation and limit the workweek to five days, rather than six, the standard at the time. She even established a social aid system for her staff.

The Melitta brand is still a household name and has expanded into other products with more than a thousand registered patents. And while you can find her coffee filters on most grocery shelves, our criterion for what makes a good cup of coffee—clean, balanced, free of errant grounds—still reflects her vision over a century ago for a better cup.

ERNA KNUTSEN Since 2000, we've been riding the third wave of coffee culture, an era in which discerning consumers take extreme care with their coffee, seeking a greater appreciation not only for their brew but also the supply chain, from source to very last sip. Coffee aficionados owe it all to the Grande Dame of Coffee, Erna Knutsen, who introduced "specialty coffee"—and coined the phrase—back in 1974. She immigrated to the United States from Norway, and in the 1960s, Erna was working as a secretary for a coffee trader at a time when women weren't even allowed in "cupping" rooms, where coffee was examined for quality control, let alone thought competent enough to sell the stuff. But Erna loved coffee passionately and fought her way into the boys' club: transitioning from secretary to a respected saleswoman, launching her own importing business, and co-founding the Specialty Coffee Association of America to preserve traditional small-batch production.

It would be impossible to imagine a world in which corner coffee shops could exist without the care for coffee Erna modeled, and women in the coffee world have been empowered to fight for positions throughout the supply chain thanks to her efforts.

AIDA BATLLE Aida Batlle produces the award-winning Finca Kilimanjaro coffee, considered among the best in the world. A fifth-generation coffee farmer, she grew up in the United States but returned to El Salvador to run the family coffee farm. She eschewed the common practice of growing coffee for speed and yield rather than flavor. Bringing home the philosophy of farm-to-table, or in this case farm-to-cup, production, Aida focused on quality and sustainable farming practices. And she worked to provide safe, financially advantageous conditions for her workers. She is the first woman ever to win the Alliance for Coffee Excellence's Cup of Excellence, a highly competitive international award for the world's best producer.

Clara Steele

1823–1866

WHEN CLARA STEELE and her family left their native Ohio for the great frontier in the nineteenth century, Clara couldn't have known her passionate love of cheese would alter not only her own fate, but the agricultural identity of an entire state—and spread like Velveeta around the country.

Spanish missionaries are credited with bringing soft, creamy cheese—*queso del pais*, the forebear of Monterey Jack—to the Golden State and teaching natives to make it. But American settlers brought their love of curds to California during the dairy boom of 1848, a by-product of the California Gold Rush. As the frenzy to strike it rich prompted pioneers to make the trek

west, many realized that it was more lucrative to supply food to hopeful miners. Milk became liquid gold. Dairy's high prices motivated businessmen to import thousands of dairy cows, boosting the local production of a sought-after commodity: butter. Women were charged with tending to cattle and made soft farmer's cheese and cottage cheese, which they sold on their homesteads. But amid this boom, hard, ripe cheeses were still difficult to come by; the ones available were imported and degraded in quality. That is, until Clara and her family came along.

Clara missed her grandmother's cheddar. Determined to re-create it in her new home, she started making the cheese according to her grandmother's recipe. Fortunately for us, she didn't keep it to herself. She was so pleased with her hard cheese that she took it to the San Francisco market, where the public snapped it up. Inspired, her husband and his cousins launched Steele Brothers Dairy, producing fine cheese and butter. Though the enterprise was named for the men in her life, Clara's work was the foundation of the first commercial dairy in the United States.

In 1857, her family expanded their production, establishing a six-thousand-acre dairy in Point Reyes. Four years later, they produced the highest volume of cheese in California. A simple yearning for a sense of home and one woman's love of cheese were the basis for generations of Steele family success. But it was Clara's entrepreneurial spirit that sparked a multi-billion-dollar industry.

Women
BEHIND YOUR
Favorite Foods
MULTIPLE ERAS

MUMTAZ MAHAL AND BIRYANI Though several legends exist about the creation of the Indian favorite, according to one interpretation it was Mumtaz Mahal, empress and wife of the fifth Mughal emperor, Shah Jahan, who can be credited with the first biryani. In the seventeenth century, Mumtaz was troubled when she visited military barracks and found her soldiers weak and malnourished. She called on her chef to create a dish that could be whipped up fast and would pack nutritional punch. A sauté of rice, meats, vegetables, and ghee, biryani is a fully balanced meal that, as evidenced by its enduring appeal, is also very delicious.

JULIA DAVIS CHANDLER AND THE PEANUT BUTTER AND JELLY SANDWICH There is perhaps no more iconic epicurean bedfellow than the PB&J, but in the late nineteenth century, peanut butter was paired with less familiar partners, like pimento cheese. Thankfully, Julia Davis Chandler's cookbook, published in 1901, nearly thirty years before the first sale of sliced bread, included the first printed recipe for the sando we love today. Her version calls for currant or crab apple jelly, which may not be exactly what we recall from cafeteria tables, but still inspired lunch boxes for generations to come.

RUTH GRAVES WAKEFIELD AND THE CHOCOLATE CHIP COOKIE A dietitian and lecturer, Ruth was no stranger to the kitchen when she and her husband purchased the Toll House Inn in Massachusetts in 1930. She became a culinary legend when she added chunks of a Nestlé semisweet chocolate bar to the dough and the Toll House cookie was born. After Ruth featured the cookie in her wildly successful cookbook, *Toll House Tried and True Recipes*, it became so famous that Nestlé purchased the recipe, which lives on the back of every yellow Nestlé Semi-Sweet Morsels package to this day. Similar cookie confections may have existed before her, but we have Ruth to thank for perfecting and proliferating her version, making her recipe the global standard.

TERESSA BELLISSIMO AND BUFFALO WINGS Since they were first served in 1964 at the Anchor Bar in Buffalo, New York, there have been competing theories about how Teressa Bellissimo was inspired to create her first batch of buffalo wings. She may have been improvising a snack for her son and his hungry college friends, or for Catholic patrons who, late on a Friday night, had been abstaining from meat and needed something to pair with a post-midnight beer. Or maybe she needed to use up an unexpected delivery of chicken wings. No matter the real reason, when Teressa deep-fried those flappers, smothered them with a spicy sauce of her own concocting, and served them with celery sticks and blue cheese dressing, a classic American dish took flight.

EMELINE JONES AND THE POTATO CHIP Though a cook named George Crum is often credited with inventing the potato chip, there is evidence to suggest it may have been Emeline Jones—or that, at the very least, she was the chef to popularize them. Emeline was born a slave in Maryland but gained her freedom in 1860, when she moved to New York. She worked as a cook at Moon's Lake House in Saratoga, where Crum had also worked and the potato chip is said to have been born. Emeline lived in Manhattan and became a successful caterer. Her obituary credited her as "the originator of the Saratoga chips," but her terrapin stew—an unusual and expensive dish—also made her a favorite of the wealthy and elite, including Presidents Chester Arthur and Grover Cleveland. From the humble potato chip to the haute cuisine of her day, Emeline left a lasting mark on popular food.

ELIZABETH GREGORY AND THE MODERN-DAY DOUGHNUT So essential to the human spirit is a morsel of sweet fried dough that something resembling a doughnut can be traced to ancient times. But for the doughnut as we know it today, we have a New England woman named Elizabeth Gregory to thank. Her son—a sea captain—is often given credit for inventing the modern doughnut when in fact it was Elizabeth who prepared the cakes for his long journeys. The signature hole, however, may indeed be Captain Gregory's contribution: the story goes that he added the opening so he could hang the cakes from the handles of his ship's wheel.

MARY RANDOLPH AND MAC AND CHEESE The earliest evidence of combining cheese with pasta comes—perhaps not surprisingly—from Italy, where a recipe for pasta cooked with grated cheese was published in the thirteenth century. The credit for the boxed mac Americans love often goes to Thomas Jefferson, who returned from a trip to Europe raving about a dish of pasta-and-cheese "pie" or "pudding." Some historians suspect the recipe was actually the invention of James Hemings, Jefferson's enslaved cook and a gourmet chef. But Mary Randolph, the White House's hostess following the death of Jefferson's wife, published a recipe for "macaroni" made with a nondescript cheese and butter in her 1824 cookbook, *The Virginia Housewife*, giving us the basis for all those blue boxes, and the truffled, lobster-laced, and other interpretations today.

BAKED BROWN BUTTER LEMON DOUGHNUTS WITH LEMON HAZELNUT GLAZE

MAKES 12 DOUGHNUTS

EQUIPMENT: 2 standard doughnut pans or baking sheet, parchment paper, and pastry bag or quart-sized freezer bag with tip cut off

BAKED BROWN BUTTER LEMON DOUGHNUTS

6 tablespoons unsalted butter

2 cups cake or pastry flour, sifted

1½ teaspoons baking powder

½ teaspoon baking soda

¼ teaspoon kosher salt

½ cup turbinado sugar

½ cup dark brown sugar

Zest of 1 lemon

2 eggs

1 cup whole milk

LEMON HAZELNUT GLAZE

2 tablespoons unsalted butter, melted

1 cup confectioners' sugar

1 tablespoon fresh lemon juice

1 tablespoon water

1 teaspoon pure vanilla extract

½ cup toasted hazelnuts, finely chopped

Make the Baked Brown Butter Lemon Doughnuts: Preheat oven to 375°F.

Grease doughnut pan or line baking sheet with parchment paper if piping doughnuts by hand.

Place butter in saucepan over medium heat. Stir occasionally while butter melts and foams. Once milk solids start to brown on bottom of pan, scrape them to loosen and remove pan from heat. Immediately pour butter and brown bits into small bowl. Let cool completely.

To measure flour, use spoon to fill measuring cup loosely and then level with knife. In large mixing bowl, combine flour, baking powder, baking soda, salt, sugars, and lemon zest. Whisk to combine. In separate bowl or measuring cup,

whisk eggs, milk, and cooled brown butter. Add wet ingredients to dry ingredients, folding batter until just combined and no dry ingredients or lumps are visible.

Spoon batter into greased doughnut pan, filling only three-quarters full. If piping batter, stagger 3-inch circles on baking sheet lined with parchment paper to allow room for doughnuts to expand. Bake for 10 minutes, until golden brown and toothpick inserted in doughnuts comes out clean.

Make the Lemon Hazelnut Glaze: Combine melted butter, confectioners' sugar, lemon juice, water, and vanilla in mixing bowl. Whisk until smooth. Dip one side of cooled doughnuts into glaze, letting excess drip off, and place on wire rack. Generously sprinkle with chopped hazelnuts and let glaze dry completely.

Enjoy doughnuts the same day or store overnight in brown paper bag in cool, dry place.

Josephine Cochrane

1839 - 1913

T HE DISHES AREN'T GOING TO do themselves. But thanks to the ingenuity of one woman, we do have a machine that does them for us.
Josephine Cochrane's invention of the automatic dishwasher immediately
transformed the hospitality industry of her day. It also went on to change
the lives of women in the kitchen for generations, returning precious hours
to their days and giving them the freedom to pursue goals outside the home.

Josephine was born in 1839 in Ohio. When she married William A.
Cochran, a merchant and county clerk, at the age of twenty-seven, she
became the hostess of the lavish dinner parties he threw for his colleagues in
their Indiana mansion. She played the dutiful entertainer but was frustrated
by the frequency with which their china was chipped and broken during
cleanup. She decided to relieve their servants of the duty and do the washing
herself, but the task was tedious, and she quickly tired of it. There had to be
a better way.

Perhaps it was her upbringing that gave her the gumption to undertake an engineering effort unthinkable for a woman of her day. She was an independent, highly educated, and well-connected woman with the time and resources to spare. She began tinkering with designs, but after William passed away in 1883 and left her with substantial debt, what started as a passion project became a potential livelihood—and a priority.

Josephine engaged George Butters, a local mechanic for the Illinois Central Railroad, to assist in bringing her vision to life and introduced the machine at the 1893 Chicago World's Fair. In a patent issued in December 1886, she made a declaration: "Be it known that I, JOSEPHINE G. COOHRANE [sic]...have invented certain new and useful Improvements in Dish-Washing Machines." Her early models were large and costly, ill suited for the home. So she sold her first machines to hotels and restaurants—including prestigious institutions like Chicago's Sherman House and Palmer House. Josephine continued to refine and streamline, always with the aim of making her creation more accessible, marketable, and efficient. She didn't create just the dishwasher, but also a business empire and a household name. Her Garis-Cochran DishWashing Company was acquired by the Hobart Company, which went on to sell the machine under another name: KitchenAid.

While she wouldn't be alive to see the mass proliferation of the dishwasher, by the 1950s her invention was an essential part of the modern home thanks to advances in technology in the early twentieth century that made the appliance practical for the home user. Like the convenience foods, like boxed cake mixes, and other time-saving devices that emerged at the time, dishwashers did more than keep women's hands clean in the kitchen; they helped liberate them. And ladies found all sorts of ways to spend that time: starting a new job outside the home, joining a bridge club, or even finding their political voice (it's no coincidence that a new wave of feminist thinking shortly followed). The dishwasher was a small but mighty part of a major change.

Amanda Jones

1835–1914

*T*O COOK IS HUMAN, to preserve divine. And if it seems like there's something miraculous about keeping food fresh long after its time, well, there might be a good reason for that. Amanda Jones claimed that divine inspiration helped her dream up the vacuum canning process in the late nineteenth century.

Born in New York, Amanda worked in her early years as a teacher. But after a bout with tuberculosis left her physically impaired—and perhaps in part because of her near-death experience with the disease—she decided to abandon the more practical field of teaching to pursue her passion, poetry. Amanda became active in the Spiritualist movement of the time, and thanks to suggestions straight from the other side, she also became an inventor.

In her autobiography, Amanda thanked a number of advisers who helped spur her research and innovations. Many of whom, it just so happened, were dead at the time. In fact, she claimed that her deceased brother communicated with her from beyond the grave and suggested she improve on the process of fruit preservation. Because what else would be on the minds of the dearly departed but new ways to keep something wonderful alive?

Canning and preserving were not new to the culinary world, but they became more common following the development of pasteurization in 1864. The problem was, much canned food was cooked before packaging, which degraded the flavor and texture, and in some cases required chemical additives. After rigorous testing and experimentation, Amanda found a way to remove the air from within the can without first cooking the ingredients. She ultimately was awarded five patents, two individually and three jointly, for her work in food preservation.

In 1890, she opened the Women's Canning and Preserving Company, a business entirely run by women. Amanda was steadfast and explicit in her feminist goals; she declared hers was a "woman's industry. No man will vote our stock, transact our business, pronounce on women's wages, or supervise our factories. Give men whatever work is suitable, but keep the governing power." Unfortunately, the business was not destined to last, but though the doors closed, Amanda's patents revolutionized the way we store, ship, sell, serve, and enjoy food. Regardless of her spiritual path, her business demonstrated that above all, there was one tangible thing Amanda truly believed in: the power of women.

Women of Cooking Schools

NINETEENTH AND TWENTIETH CENTURIES

FANNIE FARMER AND MISS FARMER'S SCHOOL OF COOKERY Bakers of the world, raise your cakes to Fannie Farmer. In 1896, she provided one of the greatest gifts to the precision-obsessed: the modern recipe and its accurate measurements.

Measuring cups and spoons were around during Fannie's time, but few recipes called for a standard measurement, instead using a "palm-full" of this or "a little" of that. Fannie was the first to prove the importance of proper

FRANCES ROTH

KATHERINE ANGELL

FANNIE FARMER

FLOUR

THE BOSTON COOKING SCHOOL COOKBOOK

DOROTHY CANN HAMILTON

measurements. After a paralytic stroke in high school dashed her collegiate dreams, she took up work as a mother's helper for a wealthy family, who encouraged her to attend the Boston Cooking School. She enrolled at thirty-one, immersing herself in the science behind food and cooking, including nutrition, housekeeping, and sanitation. After graduation, she taught at her alma mater and became the principal five years later. She was a respected authority on diet and health, and lectured at Harvard Medical School—one of the first women to do so. In 1896, she published *The Boston Cooking-School Cookbook*, now known as *The Fannie Farmer Cookbook*, and her exact, clear recipes were an instant success. The classic has sold millions of copies and is still considered one of the most important cookbooks of the twentieth century.

In 1902, Fannie started her own cooking school, Miss Farmer's School of Cookery, a lucrative business that gave women the confidence to whip up a meal without stress, as her guidance and instruction removed the guess-work from cooking. Thanks to Fannie, modern cooks still take comfort that with a good recipe, anyone can create with certainty.

FRANCES ROTH AND KATHERINE ANGELL AND THE CULINARY INSTITUTE OF AMERICA In 1946, two women joined forces to create one of the most prestigious culinary schools in the world. Neither had ever cooked professionally. Frances Roth was actually a trailblazer in the field of law, one of the first women members of the Connecticut Bar Association. Frances noticed that many restaurant kitchens were extremely short-staffed following World War II, which meant job opportunities for returning veterans. But first they needed training as chefs. She recruited a powerhouse partner, Katherine, and the New Haven Restaurant Institute was born.

Katherine Angell had excellent fund-raising skills and knew the inner workings of higher education, as the wife of Yale University's president. She was integral in building the school's culinary library and relocated the school closer to Yale. In 1951, she and Frances changed its name to the Culinary Institute of America, reflecting a national reach and increasing diversity of students. Frances went to Congress to fight for the school's accreditation as a bona fide university and not a trade school, and in 1971, the CIA became the first school of its kind to offer an associate in occupational studies degree. Frances served as president of the school for nearly two decades.

Many CIA graduates have become luminaries of the cooking world, Anthony Bourdain, Grant Achatz, Cat Cora, and Sara Moulton among them. And in March 2017, for the first time in the institute's history, female enrollment surpassed that of men.

DOROTHY CANN HAMILTON AND THE INTERNATIONAL CULINARY CENTER Bobby Flay, Dan Barber, David Chang, Christina Tosi, and Wylie Dufresne—all began their culinary journey at the school founded by Dorothy Cann Hamilton. A passionate educator, Dorothy loved food despite a limited academic knowledge of gastronomy. Her university education in England, and food-centric jaunts to France, introduced her to "a life beyond Velveeta," as a friend recalled in the *New York Times*. She dreamed of opening a restaurant, but her plan took an unexpected turn. Dorothy paid a visit to several vocational institutions in Paris as a board member of the National Association of Trade and Technical Schools. She was amazed by the quality of these schools for professional chefs and decided to establish her own: the French Culinary Institute in New York—now known as the International Culinary Center.

Basing its curriculum on French techniques, the school opened in 1984 in Manhattan's SoHo neighborhood to a quiet reception. So when Dorothy received a call that Julia Child wanted to have a meal prepared by her students, she knew she couldn't pass up the chance. Dorothy, her chef instructor, and her students presented an elegant lunch prepared the French way to Julia and her friends, including a producer from *Good Morning America*. The meal led to a feature about the school on *GMA* and brought it to national prominence.

Dorothy had the foresight to bring on the best in the industry as teachers, culinary giants like Jacques Pépin, André Soltner, Jacques Torres, Alain Sailhac, José Andrés, Nils Norén, and Cesare Casella. Her school expanded to include other international cuisines, and she changed the name to the International Culinary Center to reflect these influences.

Dorothy received the Legion of Honor from the French government for promoting French cuisine at home in the United States, an award previously given to only three other American recipients: Julia Child, Thomas Keller, and Alice Waters. Dorothy championed thousands of students, helping them to attain a solid culinary foundation.

Sister Mary of Jesus de Ágreda and the San Antonio Chili Queens

SEVENTEENTH, NINETEENTH, AND TWENTIETH CENTURIES

A BOWL OF SPICY, CHEESY, and hearty chili on a cold day can provide a pleasure bordering on the spiritual, and the origins of the hot dish may actually have been divine. In the early seventeenth century, Sister Mary of Jesus de Ágreda was stationed at a convent in Spain. And while she never left her home country in the physical sense, Sister Mary went into regular

trances in which she reported being transported across the Atlantic to Texas and the American Southwest. During one of these spells, it is said, she awoke with a recipe for a pepper-spiked stew made with venison, onions, tomato, and peppers. The dish was essentially what we know as chili con carne, apparently heaven-sent.

Several centuries later, a similar dish was setting the food world on fire in America. Shortly after the Civil War, in Texas, the land that Sister Mary once visited in her visions, markets sprang up in San Antonio's open-air plazas. They were the city's centers of community and commerce, and there women set up stalls from which to sell food to local laborers. One especially popular dish was tamales with beans and chili.

Though originally intended to feed poor workers who frequented the market, thanks to wealthier travelers making their way through town, including the writers and poets who documented their meals, the market's food started to capture the attention and appetites of all. The interest in Mexican food that followed was a great equalizer for a culturally and economically divided community ravaged by war. And at the center of it all? Great big bowls of chili.

The fierce businesswomen who brought their specialty to the market became known as the San Antonio Chili Queens. And as travelers passed through and new populations came to settle in San Antonio and surrounding areas, the taste for their spicy food exploded, helping Tex-Mex become a popular and uniquely American cuisine. Eventually, changes to the community slowed the Chili Queens' influence, and the institution of health regulations ultimately ended their reign. But so beloved is the memory of this former version of royalty that today the city hosts an annual Return of the Chili Queens Festival, which features live music, arts and crafts, and a chili cook-off.

SWEET AND SPICY BEER CHILI

SERVES 6 TO 8

EQUIPMENT: 4½-quart Dutch oven or large stockpot

¼ cup olive oil, divided

2 pounds ground turkey

1 teaspoon kosher salt

½ teaspoon cracked black pepper

1 small red onion, diced

2 shallots, diced

1 tablespoon garlic, minced

1 pint (16 ounces) dark beer (such as Negra Modelo or dunkel)

1 cup chicken stock

½ cup tomato juice

1 tablespoon tomato paste

1 (14½-ounce) can peeled tomatoes, diced

¼ cup honey

2 tablespoons canned, diced Hatch chiles

2 chipotle peppers in adobo sauce, plus 1 tablespoon sauce

1 hot chili pepper (such as serrano or jalapeño), seeded and diced

1 tablespoon unsweetened cocoa

1 tablespoon ground cumin

½ teaspoon kosher salt

¼ teaspoon ground cinnamon

¼ teaspoon ground allspice

2 (15-ounce) cans beans (kidney, pinto, black beans, or a combination)

1 lime, halved

Heat half the oil in Dutch oven or large stockpot set over medium heat. Add turkey, salt, and pepper, and sauté until meat is slightly browned. Remove from pot and set aside. Add remaining oil and sauté onion, shallots, and garlic until translucent. Add beer, chicken stock, tomato juice, and tomato paste. Stir to combine.

Add tomatoes, honey, chiles, chipotle peppers and adobo sauce, chili pepper, remaining dry ingredients, beans, and sautéed turkey. Cover partially and simmer over low heat for 1½ hours, stirring occasionally, until thickened. Ladle into bowls and finish with squeeze of lime juice.

Garnish with cilantro, scallions, or fresh avocado slices. Serve with warm corn tortillas or cornbread.

Further Reading

Hungry for more culinary cultural history? These books
are a fantastic place to start.

Lady Eve Balfour, *The Living Soil*

Hattie Burr, *The Woman Suffrage Cook Book: Containing Thoroughly Tested and Reliable Recipes for Cooking, Directions for the Care of the Sick, and Practical Suggestions, Contributed Especially for This Work*

Elizabeth David, *A Book of Mediterranean Food* and *Italian Food*

M.F.K. Fisher, *The Gastronomical Me*

Maria Grammatico and Mary Taylor Simeti, *Bitter Almonds: Recollections and Recipes from a Sicilian Girlhood*

Dorothy Cann Hamilton with Lisa Cornelio and Christopher Papagni, *Love What You Do: Building a Career in the Culinary Industry*

Madhur Jaffrey, *An Invitation to Indian Cooking*

Judith Jones, *The Pleasures of Cooking for One* and *The Tenth Muse: My Life in Food*

Edna Lewis, *The Taste of Country Cooking*

Tilar J. Mazzeo, *The Widow Clicquot: The Story of a Champagne Empire and the Woman Who Ruled It*

Fred Minnick, *Whiskey Women: The Untold Story of How Women Saved Bourbon, Scotch, and Irish Whiskey*

Sidney W. Mintz, *Sweetness and Power: The Place of Sugar in Modern History*

Mary Seacole, *Wonderful Adventures of Mrs. Seacole in Many Lands*

Vertamae Smart-Grosvenor, *Vibration Cooking: or, The Travel Notes of a Geechee Girl*

Isabel Stilwell, *Catherine of Braganza: The Courage of a Portuguese Infanta Who Became Queen of England*

Brenda Paik Sunoo with Youngsook Han, *Moon Tides: Jeju Island Grannies of the Sea*

Ruth Graves Wakefield, *Toll House Tried and True Recipes*

Acknowledgments

To Nicky Guerreiro and Michael Szczerban, for your vision, support, attentiveness, and encouraging words. You helped us take a humble idea and turn it into something totally magical. We couldn't possibly have dreamed up a team of editors more perfectly suited for this project—and ones we now happily consider friends.

And special thanks to Nicky for your title skills, too.

To our copyeditors, Jayne Yaffe Kemp and Deborah P. Jacobs, for making our words shine. Thanks to Laura Palese for the outstanding design of our book, and to the entire Little, Brown production team for working so hard to make *A Woman's Place* a reality.

To Jessica Olah, for your collaboration, open mind, and killer talent in creating these beautiful images. Your passion helped keep us animated, and your illustrations brought our dream to life.

DEEPI WOULD LIKE TO THANK

My partner and fellow KIND Bar addict, Stef, for sharing this incredible journey with me. Through our coffee-and-candy-fueled ride, you kept things cool and calm. Thanks for the laughs, thousands of texts, and for being so damn smart. Your friendship and trust are a true gift. I aspire to write as fast as you one day, Dash! I love you, dude.

My mother for patiently showing me the ins and outs of the kitchen, and for instilling in me the importance of honesty, kindness, and hard work. Mom, no words can fully express how much I love and respect you. You have been my lifeline, and my career would not be possible without you.

Sandeep, the most encouraging husband on the planet, for all the delicious dinners, tea and coffee refills, and countless hours entertaining P. and S. while I worked. You are my constant champion. I love you.

The two halves of my heart, Paavni and Suhaavi, for the endless giggles and distractions, and the daily reminder that being your mama is the greatest joy and accomplishment of my life.

My awesome bro, Harp, for being my biggest cheerleader, keeping my coolness in check, and never treating me "like a girl." I couldn't have asked for a better sibling.

To those who are no longer here but their love remains: my father and nani.

Mummy Ji, Daddy Ji, Jo Bhen Ji, Manpreet, Ishdeep, Neetu, Franz, Mehar, Saachi, and Mehma for your love, support, and blessings. And for being such enthusiastic taste testers.

Jatinder Mama Ji for your unconditional love.

Jigisha Bouverat for your wisdom and friendship, and for always having my back. To the JBC ladies—Sonia, Marni, and Ginger—for your boundless, kickass enthusiasm. I heart you all.

Antonio Diaz and *Life & Thyme* for encouraging me to pursue culturally significant stories, giving my culinary writing a home, and for supporting female talent both behind the scenes and in the spotlight. AD, much love and respect for these opportunities. And to

the ladies of Doyenne: the fire was lit and you responded. You will forever be a force in food.

To all the amazing women in this book. Your stories fed my curiosity, opened my heart, and nourished my soul, and I am a better person for it. You paved roads for all of us currently in kitchens, running businesses, writing and capturing food stories, and inventing ways to improve culinary lives. Thank you for fighting for what is rightfully ours.

And finally, to the Universal Truth for guiding my work.

STEF WOULD LIKE TO THANK

Deepi. How can I count the ways? For being a fiercely passionate creative partner and a constant source of inspiration—professionally and personally. For sharing with me your talent, your grace, your time, and, above all, your friendship, thank you. Only you and I will ever know the laughter and tears (and coffee, KIND Bars, and packs of gum) that went into making this crazy thing. There's a bottle of almond wine and a Sicilian sunset with our names on them.

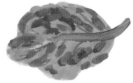

Mollie Glick, for being my champion and a true friend, a sounding board and a sound adviser. I have learned so much from you. I hope I can return the generosity somehow, even if only in scoops of ice cream. And to Ben, Gabe, and Griff for just being the coolest.

Farrin Jacobs, for cocktails dates and surprise deliveries of cookies and ice cream. For the constant advice, and for being the one to say (over a dish of *cacio e pepe*), "That's a book. Do that." I am eternally grateful for your generous guidance and your friendship. And to Paula, of course.

Rose and Kev Pryor. There are just no words. Sure, you're the best damn parents a kid could ask for, but you're also my best friends, and my true north.

Tina Ferrari, for showing me the importance of a tablecloth, conversations over figs and *pizza al taglio*, for the fresh-squeezed OJ, high-quality hugs, and my Italian office space.

Nonny and Grandpa, for teaching me the significance of history, and where we came from. Heather and Ava, for being a window into the future.

The Ahluwalia family, for sharing Deepi; I know how much she was missed.

Antonio Diaz for your endless advocacy for a female presence in this industry; Gia Hughes for being one of the most inspiring women I've ever known; Ben Hunter for your thoughtful insights and pure heart.

Cash Langford for your ear and your kindness. Selina, Dale, and the crew at East One for endless cortados, and for not kicking me out when you probably should have.

Katie Bell, the Andys, and Brian and Ashley Ewing for your excitement, Champagne toasts, and pizza, and the conversations that keep me inspired.

Maite Gomez-Rejon for your knowledge and passion.

The women in this book, for paving the way so that people like Deepi and me get to do what we do.

To the women of Doyenne for your time, participation, and your leadership.

And to all the women in this industry today, who make strides against stacked odds so future generations can find their voice, who continue to make sure that those who want one will always have a place in the kitchen.

Index

About the Authors

DEEPI AHLUWALIA is a food writer and photographer and a columnist for *Life & Thyme* magazine. She has worked with such brands, companies, and publications as American Airlines, Nestlé, JCPenney, the *Dallas Morning News*, Jacques Torres Chocolate, and Walmart. She holds a degree in pastry arts from the French Culinary Institute.

STEF FERRARI is senior editor of *Life & Thyme* magazine. She is an Emmy-winning, James Beard Foundation Award–nominated producer on the documentary series *The Migrant Kitchen*, which explores the influence of immigrant culture on America's foodways. Her recipes have been featured in *O, The Oprah Magazine*, *Better Homes and Gardens*, and *Southern Living*, and she has appeared on the Food Network's *Cutthroat Kitchen* and *Unique Sweets*.